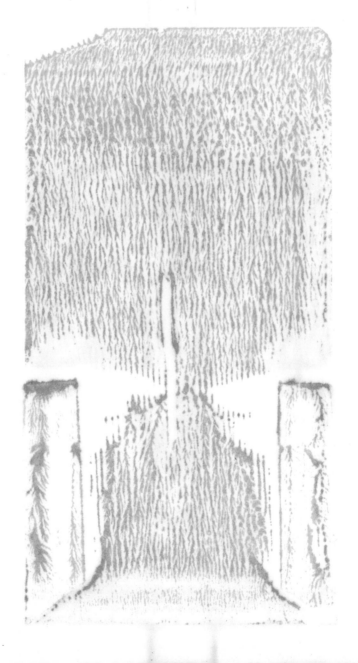

The
Treasury
Of
New England
Antiques

Also by George Michael

Antiquing with George Michael

The Treasury Of New England Antiques

by George Michael

HAWTHORN BOOKS, INC.

Publishers/New York

2 3 4 5 6 7 8 9 10

This book is dedicated to my wife,
BETTE,
whose enthusiastic reception to every
new acquisition for our home is
reason enough to be associated
with antiques.

Contents

Introduction   ix

CHAPTER 1 Why Antiques and Why in New England?   1

CHAPTER 2 Furniture   9

CHAPTER 3 Glass   55

CHAPTER 4 Earthenware and Porcelain   80

CHAPTER 5 Clocks   99

CHAPTER 6 Silver, Iron, Copper, Tin, Pewter, and Brass   111

CHAPTER 7 Dolls and Children's Artifacts   134

CHAPTER 8 Oils, Lithographs, and Prints   146

CHAPTER 9 Other Collectible Items   156

CHAPTER 10 Tips on Buying Antiques   170

Index   187

Introduction

PEOPLE like to shop for antiques in New England because this area is one of the few remaining storehouses of our early artifacts. During the summer it is exciting fun to browse through old shop-barns and go to country auctions. There are still many grandmothers' attics to be emptied; and buyers, hoping to be at the right place at the right time, are lured from all over the country.

My old traveling partner, Frank Rowe, showed me another reason why antiquers like to go to New England—to meet the people who buy and sell antiques. New England has a colorful heritage, and its taciturn inhabitants are accustomed to outsiders who return year after year, delighting in the old traditions that have remained alive.

For ten years Frank led me to old farmhouses with their rewarding attics and barns. He had a knack for discovering hidden objects. He seemed to know which board to lift in a barn floor to reveal old bottles or an ox yoke. Secret shelves, unknown even to their owners, that were built overhead and to the front of cupboards, quite often held interesting objects. Among barn rafters covered with hay he would find old chamber pots, oil lamps, and other objects stored there and forgotten many years ago. Once, the owner of a farm, piqued by an offer Frank had made on a handsome art-glass pitcher, threw it into his well, saying that no one would ever own it at that price. When the farmer died, and I, with the new owner's permission, went searching in the well, Frank's perseverance paid off. We hooked the handle of the pitcher, and, to the amazement of all, up it came, totally unharmed by its long immersion.

Frank taught me to enjoy the people who dealt in antiques as much as the objects themselves. Antiquing should be fun, and if you approach it with this in mind, you are bound to be richly rewarded.

I should like to thank the following people, who have given generously of their time, advice, and illustrative material, to make this book possible: Richard Carter Barret, Director-Curator, Bennington Museum, Bennington, Vermont; Philip Hammerslough, West Hartford, Connecticut; W. Bradley Smith, Curator, Shelburne Museum, Shelburne, Vermont; Joseph Bates, British clockmaker, Newfane, Vermont; Charles Parsons, historian, Goffstown, New Hampshire; Marie S. Quick, Director, The Holyoke Museum of Natural History and Art, Holyoke, Massachusetts; David S. Brooke, Director, and Melvin Watts, Curator, Currier Gallery of Art, Manchester, New Hampshire; Gerald C. Stowe, Curator, West Point Museum; Mrs. F. L. Schmidt, Director, First Iron Works Association, Saugus, Massachusetts; Mr. and Mrs. E. L. Davis, Riverside, Rhode Island; John Pancoast, Curator, and Miss Marion Dana, of the Portland Museum of Art, Portland, Maine; Ruth and Kenneth Wakefield, West Duxbury, Massachusetts; Louis Joseph, Boston, Massachusetts; Geraldine Sanderson, Museum of Fine Arts, Boston, Massachusetts.

Excerpts from articles that have appeared in the *New England Homestead* magazine and *New Hampshire Profiles* magazine have been reproduced with permission. Material concerning the unusual secretary-chest in the Warner House in Portsmouth, New Hampshire, has been excerpted from an article that originally appeared in the *Christian Science Monitor*. It is used by permission from the *Christian Science Monitor*, © 1968, the Christian Science Publishing Company, all rights reserved.

GEORGE MICHAEL

Reeds Ferry, New Hampshire

The
Treasury
Of
New England
Antiques

CHAPTER 1

Why Antiques and Why in New England?

To BORROW from Winston Churchill, "Never has so small an area contributed so much to so many." Weathered New England farmhouses by country roads yield up their antiques as dealers make their rounds. Country auctions, once an enterprise confined to the warmer months, have become a year-round way of life. Shortly after World War II, auction barns flourished, and began operating fifty-two weeks a year. Antique dealers, who had been in the habit of closing up in October, after the tourists left, learned they could continue to do a booming business, particularly at Christmas, which is an excellent occasion to give antiques. Flea markets and antique shows now run all winter long, generally on weekends, in halls, convention rooms, at motels, and in church meeting rooms.

The prices of finer antiques have risen so high that today collectors often settle for items they might never have dreamed of buying just a few years ago. As recently as 1960, buyers were highly concerned about condition and style. A repaired leg, new brasses, or slightly cut-down legs, factors that would alter style and proportions, would send a piece to an auction consignment to fetch what little it could. Today, if a piece is merely authentic, it is accepted with very little question.

While there is evidence that New England had visitors long before Columbus and the Pilgrims, these people left mainly some rock piles (thought to be grave mounds) in Rhode Island. As for the American Indian, in the New England area collecting seems to consist of arrowheads, tomahawk heads, and bits and pieces of pottery. In searching out the artifacts and art of this area, we must begin with the period directly following the landing of the Pilgrims in 1620.

If every piece of furniture and household utensil said to be cargo on the first *Mayflower* voyage really was on that vessel, the *Mayflower* would never have left the dock. This points out the importance of proper documentation. One has only to visit the present-day reconstruction of the *Mayflower* at Plymouth, Massachusetts, to realize that the passengers were cramped for space, and must have concentrated on storing food, clothing, bedding, and small hand tools rather than pots, pans, and furniture. Too many carved oak chests, Carver-type chairs, and slant-top desks have miraculously turned out to be passengers on this first voyage. If you are obsessed with owning a *Mayflower* piece, be patient—one will turn up.

The Pilgrims sought out the soft pine trees, an easy wood to handle with crude tools, and supplied themselves with the necessities of furniture, which we appropriately call "Pilgrim" pieces. Hardwoods, such as oak, maple, and birch were also used, as well as some elm, ash, chestnut, and beech. But the major sources were pine and oak.

The Saugus Iron Works, just a short distance north of Boston, began operating in 1646, using the bog iron from the nearby Saugus marshes. Native clays were used for pottery, but several crude attempts at window glass met with failure. About the only artifacts that survived this period for us to collect and enjoy are the pieces of Pilgrim furniture, some of which are classic in their simplicity.

However, it was not until the early eighteenth century that New England craftsmanship became the equal of craftsmanship anywhere else in the world. The Queen Anne Period, which extended to about 1750, saw the development of the formal cabinetmaker's shop, with apprentices, and the hand production of what are today the most highly collectible pieces of early furniture. The William and Mary and Jacobean periods, which preceded this era, contributed furniture in quantity, yet it is the Queen Anne Period that produced the gracefully designed, finely proportioned pieces that command top prices now. Although New Englanders competed with fine craftsmen in New York, Philadelphia, and Baltimore, the excellence of the work done in New England has earned it the highest merit. Where the craftsmen from the other colonies were English-oriented in their styles and designs, the New England craftsmen created in such a distinctive manner that their work is regionally recognizable. While an appraiser may often have to spend much time determining whether an eighteenth-century piece is English or Philadelphian, a quick glance at several features can tell him if it is New England.

As we approached the nineteenth century, all kinds of handcrafts were created, and a wider range of household artifacts began to appear. New England silversmiths, pewterers, glassblowers, ironmongers, and potters broadened the industrial output of our nation. And although New England did not predate other sections of the country in effective manufacture of such items as china and glass, that which eventually came from this area won wide acceptance for its quality and design.

Foreign imports were tremendous competition. It was considered more fashionable to buy foreign goods. People felt that the workmanship was better, and because of improved production techniques Europeans were able to turn out goods at less cost and market them here for less than the native product. In addition, our own supply of raw materials was not great, for we had not yet opened our frontiers. Colonials had to import many materials, and as a result they almost had to price themselves out of the production market. England kept a tight rein on raw materials to the advantage of her own craftsmen, and would allow little or none in from other countries. Some were smuggled in aboard French and Dutch ships, and quite often a ship taken as a "prize" from pirates would be unloaded in the New World, and windfalls of gold, silver, and tin would find their way to the wealthy, and thence to the craftsmen to be made into jewelry and household dinner services and ornaments of the day.

It was only after the War of 1812 that the United States made significant strides in industrial expansion. Free trade with other nations brought in necessary supplies, and the inventive genius of our craftsmen brought about the creation of new manufacturing techniques both by hand and through new machinery. There was still competition with imported wares, and American manufacturers and tradesmen often would deliberately leave their pieces unmarked, hoping they might be mistaken for imported ones and therefore bring a better price. As a result, documentation for much of this early work is difficult to obtain. While furniture can be identified by the manner of construction and the woods used, in other fields, such as glass, pewter, and pottery, one must do considerable homework to classify unmarked pieces.

After 1892, under the McKinley Tariff Law, all imports had to be labeled with country of origin. In addition, some countries were marking all their work as early as the eighteenth century. But sometimes china that had been made long before being shipped had not been marked, and was then so marked in order to be shipped here. There also must have been much brought in unmarked by immigrants. Indeed, there are enough exceptions to the marking system to frustrate the most knowledgeable antiquarian.

That today's "trash" can become tomorrow's treasure is proved by the growing interest in "camp" antiques. Many of the items sought after today were regarded as little more than junk a few years ago, and antique dealers and auctioneers are presently enjoying a boom in selling merchandise that but a few years ago was relegated to the back of the shop or sold by the boxful at a consignment auction. Most of it is of the vintage from about 1890 and through the thirties, when furniture was made of sturdy oak and when bronzes and brass were in vogue for decoration. Designers seem to have lost their minds during the Art Nouveau Period pioneered by Louis Comfort Tiffany and his contemporaries. The use of sterile Oriental motifs was combined with garish designs in lamps, bronze figures, and carved marbles. Though furniture was then basically clumsy and awkward, it was made to last. Just try breaking up an old oak chest of drawers.

Iridescent glasses came into their own, with Tiffany leading the way and lesser makers imitating him with their bountiful carnival glass. Electric lamps with leaded oyster-shell shades became a "must" in every home. Lacking an ounce of beauty, they nevertheless were given a hallowed place in the hall for visitors to see or in the parlor where no one sat except on Sundays. Every home had a Morris chair for Father, and a heavy dining-room set that would have survived the roughest seas. The round-cornered china cupboard was often filled with Grandmother's old bits of china and glass, which were gradually pushed to the rear to make way for some Niagara Falls souvenir pieces or colorful ruby glass that the five-and-dime stores had on sale.

Some of the better kitchens had black walnut dropleaf tables with cane-seated spindle-backed chairs. And just about every kitchen had a condiment cupboard with the built-in flour sifter and work leaf that pulled out.

Iron beds with flat springs and cotton mattresses were the rule, and the occasional brass bed was considered a rich man's property. Unusual hide-a-beds were made in the shape of large chests of drawers. By lifting the top and grasping the handle of the top dummy drawer, the bed could be pulled out.

One manufacturer made a set of shelves attached to an ingenious frame that served as a shelf for china or books during the day. At suppertime one could convert it into a table by loosening a thumbscrew and pulling the top shelf backward. The shelves would remain perfectly level during the transition so that not a dish would be lost.

Pictures were set in horrible-looking frames—perhaps the reason was that the contrast between picture and frame would make the picture look better.

Washstand sets, including chamber pots, were in demand, and those with floral designs were most favored. Little spool-framed towel holders were a necessity in every home, and the many designs we see testify to the ingenuity of the makers.

Round dining tables of heavy oak cost much more than square ones. A few years ago the round ones went begging for bidders at an auction, and most ended in the woodpile. With today's craze for converting them into coffee tables, the demand far exceeds the supply.

All sorts of stone crocks, jugs, and bottles were turned out in all colors, and many had pretty animal and floral designs. These were a necessity for vinegar, molasses, and even hard cider in the country, yet today, purchased as decorative pieces, they are used mostly as lamps, vases, and cookie jars.

Iron, mahogany, and bronze lamps with tassel shades bordered on the monstrous in design, and many still find their way to the town dump —where they belong. Yet many are collected and used, apparently because some people see native charm in their unusual ugliness. Bronze clocks with reclining figures, draped and undraped, were popular in the twenties, and today their value has skyrocketed. Some people consider them very daring in concept for that period, indicating a time not quite so Victorian as some think.

Why the term "camp," and why the great interest in such objects today? Most of these items had found their way to the secondhand shops and eventually into the hands of people who were furnishing second homes or summer residences. Feeling that anything was good enough for summer use and to leave through the winter, owners would utilize their outmoded, outdated furniture and scour secondhand shops for whatever else they needed. As a result, much more of the merchandise of this period was preserved than might otherwise have been, and it keeps turning up as people "decorate" their homes.

Psychologists have several interesting theories as to why these items are so much in vogue today. A practical reason is that true antiques are rising in price so much that it is impossible for many newlyweds to consider buying them. Desiring something old and inexpensive, they acquire a taste for pieces of this vintage. There is also a theory that such pieces express a wish to rebel against conformity by emphasizing the unusual, garish, and grotesque. Another idea is that the pieces appeal to those searching for the peace and quiet of the past. Perhaps these fixtures from a bygone era give people a feeling of security and durability that today's artifacts lack. The furnishings bring back memories of childhood homes, memories of family, friends, and relatives who might have owned and prized such possessions, memories of sitting in Grandmother's rocker or setting the rung farther back on Grandfather's Morris chair to enjoy the unusual comfort of his recliner.

Whatever the reason, "camp" antiques seem here to stay, as lacking in quality as many may be.

Just a few years ago, large town houses, some individual, some attached in rows, were very inexpensive. In the older sections of some communities, many of these were rundown. Higher taxes, retired people living on fixed incomes in their old family homes, yet forced out by the inflation of our times, and the trend toward smaller contemporary designs led to the decline in appearance and value of such houses.

Today there is a rebirth of interest in these old residences. Young affluents with large families and not enough money to build new homes sufficient in size are turning to the restoration and redecoration of the old ones. In the older communities like Boston, many are built in excellent Federal style, and lend themselves to artifacts of the eighteenth and early nineteenth centuries. Communities farther west designed their homes in the later Victorian manner, with excellent materials and craftsmanship. Both can serve as a backdrop for the furniture and other items of the period, and both are in demand. Because most cities have had to lower the taxes on such residences to encourage ownership, the houses are a good buy for young families who need much living space. Most are located near churches, schools, theaters, parks, and so on, and many mothers are glad to leave the suburbs, where they were forced to act as taxi drivers for their youngsters.

The renewed interest in period homes was followed naturally by interest in the household necessities of the period; hence the search for items of the past and the soaring prices for many objects that were almost worthless years ago. A large dining room demands the large dining-room set that a few years ago was ignored at auctions. Huge mahogany and oak bedroom suites used to be burned or carted away to the town dump; but because the large bedroom in the Victorian home could not be half filled with a contemporary set, the old ones have come back.

There has been a revival of interest in old cast-iron kitchen ranges, and at least one company is making electric and gas ranges in fancy molded cast-iron designs. Round oak or walnut kitchen tables are in demand, and young mothers have found that youngsters cannot possibly damage the sturdy straight-backed kitchen chairs that go with them. Walls are torn open to reveal covered-up fireplaces, for which equipment must be bought. An old potty chair that sells for fifty cents at an auction will serve just as well as its new counterpart that sells for much more.

A large home with large bedrooms can accommodate a four-poster bed gracefully; and since the walls are bigger, pictures and mirrors are a necessity. Though a grandfather clock looks absurd in many modern homes, it is a delightful fixture in a town house. Obviously, though some of the Federal houses need the earlier furniture, this is getting much more difficult to acquire at bargain prices. Nevertheless, it is a very worthwhile investment. Many of the fine antique pieces of the Sheraton Period, and the Hepplewhite Period just before it, are still selling for less than brand-new furniture of high quality. I know a couple who purchased a fine bedroom set for nearly a thousand dollars. In ten years, that set will have depreciated to a point where it is worth only two hundred or three hundred dollars, and will bring that only because it was of good quality to begin with. The couple could have outfitted an entire bedroom with furniture of the Sheraton Period for the same money, and in ten years dealers would have begged to give them a substantial profit, despite the years of use.

If you are a younger reader beginning to set up housekeeping, and have a desire for antique furnishings, be sure to price those that you can afford, and plan your house around them. Sometimes it is almost impossible to decorate in one period alone, but it is possible to mix items in good taste. If you are in a metropolitan area and have a penchant for the larger pieces, perhaps an old town house would suit you best. In Pittsburgh there is a developer who buys old city houses, restores them to their original look, and resells them at a profit.

Elfreth's Alley in Philadelphia is a perfect example of total area restoration, even to the fire marks over the doors. Less well known but equally impressive is the Mile of History in Providence, Rhode Island, on celebrated Benefit Street. Here one may see just about every period form of architecture beautifully restored (by the Providence Restoration Society)—Federal, Early Colonial, Greek Revival, Georgian, Gothic, Victorian, Italianate Victorian, Italian Palazzo, and some built in a combination of these.

The Elmwood Avenue area in Buffalo is being redone in Bohemian style and is so colorful and interesting that it has attracted national attention. The Strawberry Banke Restoration in Portsmouth, New Hampshire, is the result of the work of a determined group of citizens who abhorred the idea of bulldozers tearing down much of the historic construction in the city. With the aid of the Federal government, they created a unique renewal program that might serve as a model for other communities that wish to save areas that may appear blighted outwardly but that actually house potential treasures.

Destruction of historic Scollay Square and the market district of Boston resulted in an irreparable loss to the city; it is the type of "urban renewal" that should never be allowed to occur. This area was almost as famous as Times Square or Piccadilly Circus. The entire Scollay Square locality could have been rehabilitated as a classic area with quaint shops, restaurants, entertainment and living quarters. The famous Old Howard Theater could have been restored as a mecca for the "off-Broadway" type of production. The old Hanover Hotel, which was once a resplendent place with character and service second to none, could easily have been brought back to life. The Crawford House might have been made ready for the modern-day Sally Keiths who helped give the old Scollay Square some of its racy flavor. In a large city such as Boston there were plenty of rundown areas with no history behind them that could have fallen to the bulldozers without loss. It is a miracle that venerable Faneuil Hall and Quincy Hall were allowed to remain, but no doubt some future generation will brand them as old buildings and call in the wrecking crews.

Olde Town in Chicago and Shadyside in Pittsburgh are always flooded with tourists, yet neither has the heritage that was torn down in Boston.

CHAPTER

2

Furniture

SOME years ago, I purchased three old tavern tables in Canada for between fifteen and twenty dollars apiece. It was like finding gold, for they were worth five or six times as much in New England. After bringing them back to New Hampshire, I called in a fellow dealer who had done much to educate me about furniture. I knew if they passed his scrutiny, all was well. He kicked one in the leg. "There's only one thing wrong with these," he muttered; "they speak French."

Suddenly, the three-board top and squared legs did not look just like the New England tables with their impressive single pine board tops and turned legs. And I erased the phrase "just like" from my vocabulary. That such a bold difference in detail could escape anyone, even a novice, is difficult to comprehend. But most newcomers to antiques do have to go through an initiation of some kind. Details that seem to confirm the authenticity of a piece become glaring differences.

Fortunately, in the area of furniture, in which New England craftsmen excelled, there are many guidelines that can make identification relatively simple. When one learns to identify crucial details, all the pieces will speak out their heritage. It is amazing that designs could be so similar, yet so unalike. We can even see differences between furniture of the northern and southern sections of New England. One must remember that in the eighteenth century Connecticut was farther away from New Hampshire by horseback than California is today by air. And since there were not very many pieces of furniture transported overland between these two states, cabinetmakers were not greatly influenced by one another's work. What is amazing is that the great majority of items

9

were sufficiently styled in the manner of the period to be easily identifiable. We know that New England cabinetmakers were influenced by English designs and by the drawings of the works of Thomas Chippendale, George Hepplewhite, and Thomas Sheraton, which were used extensively during their respective periods. It is interesting to note how New England artisans shaped these designs to their own taste and freely used native figured woods to express their artistic bent.

Woods are the best first clue to the area of origin of any piece of furniture. In New England there was extensive use of pine; all the maples, figured in tiger, curly, or bird's-eye; plain birch; light mahogany from the West Indies; and cherry where available. About 90 percent of the so-called maple furniture is really birch. It is a much more stable wood, and resists splitting and warping much better than maple. Today one of our largest manufacturers of "maple" furniture advertises that the wood is really birch, maple stained. Cherry wood was in demand for the large boards necessary for sides and tops of chests and tables, but it was rather scarce. The light mahogany contrasts with the darker shades used by the English and French. Furthermore, the Europeans were prone to varnish and stain their furniture the darker shades which were then in vogue. Abroad, the figured maples were never used, so any piece made from this wood must be of native origin. Though some walnut was used, one can generally attribute this wood to southern manufacture. Walnut was grown in abundance in Virginia, and much of it was shipped to England until the middle of the Queen Anne Period, when its quality deteriorated. We know it was used extensively, later in New York and Pennsylvania, as well as south of these states, but very little was used in New England—probably because of the cost of transporting it. Mahogany was brought here inexpensively as ballast for trading vessels. A typical voyage would take a schooner full of rum to Africa, where the cargo was sold and slaves were purchased. The slaves would then be transported to the Caribbean, where they were sold and sugar was purchased. So that the casks of sugar wouldn't shift in the ship's hold, they were stabilized with large mahogany boards and logs, which were plentiful. The sugar was then brought back to New England to make rum, when the cycle could begin again, and the mahogany found its way into the hands of ready buyers who turned it into furniture. Where the European craftsmen and many city artisans beautified their pieces with veneers and inlays, much of our native country furniture was beautified simply with the natural grain of the woods.

During the eighteenth century people were still very much English-oriented, and wealthy merchants and ship captains wanted furniture for their mansions like that in the mother country. As a result, if they did not import it, they would have it made in the same fashion, with much veneer and inlay. On the other hand, the cabinetmaker in the country was content to turn out pieces with much plainer characteristics and in proportions much more suitable to rural homes—hence the terms "city furniture" and "country furniture."

Some furniture buyers insist that everything has to be made of solid woods to be good. We hear the terms "solid mahogany," "solid maple," and so on. This is supposed to be a mark of excellence when such pieces are compared to supposedly inferior veneered work. Yet, on the whole, among antique furniture, the highly veneered and inlaid pieces generally command a much higher price. Because a good antique's value most often can be determined by the amount of handwork incorporated in its manufacture, the added work usually results in a higher price. Witness the work of the Townsends and Goddards in Rhode Island and the Seymours and Frothinghams in Boston. An exception to this rule is the work in solid tiger maple done by members of the Dunlap Circle in

Extremely fine chest-on-chest, attributed to Benjamin Frothingham, Charlestown, Massachusetts, circa 1760–1790. *Bennington Museum, Bennington, Vermont.*

Graduated drawer maple chest, by Dunlap Circle of cabinetmakers, New Hampshire, late eighteenth century. *Currier Gallery of Art, Manchester, New Hampshire*.

Tambour desk, mahogany, circa 1800. Attributed to John Seymour and Son, Boston, Massachusetts. Tambour shutters of mahogany and curly satinwood in alternating bands enclosing spaces under semielliptical arches. The cabinet interior is painted blue, which points to Seymour as the designer-manufacturer.

New Hampshire. The artisans from one family worked from 1740 to 1830, turning out the state's finest furniture pieces in solid woods. Their beauty lies in the matching and blending of wonderful grains in the woods to "decorate" the pieces without veneering. One cannot say these pieces are more beautiful—only that the technique is perhaps more demanding than that of the veneering specialist who can cover up his mistakes with a thin layer of wood.

For purposes of period identification of New England furniture, the following chart is offered:

Pilgrim or Jacobean	1620–1690
William and Mary	1690–1710
Queen Anne	1710–1750
Chippendale	1750–1775
Hepplewhite	1775–1800 ⎫ Federal
Sheraton	1800–1830 ⎭
Empire	1810–1850
Victorian	1840–1890

To evaluate them individually, we must consider the first period listed. Though we generally refer to the English-made furniture of this period

Elegant cabinet by the Seymours of Boston; secretary with interior section of china painted blue. Late eighteenth century. *Hammerslough Collection.*

as Jacobean, there is a trend on the part of historians to refer to artifacts made during this time in our country as Pilgrim pieces.

There is historical evidence that possibly John Alden was our country's first cabinetmaker—or perhaps more accurately, our country's first famous cabinetmaker. This would have been in Plymouth, near the middle of the seventeenth century. We know that our country was colonized long before the Pilgrims—in the South—and certainly there must have been work of this type done there, but little is known of it and none has survived.

Crude benches, chests, tables, and stools have been attributed to this country and era, but one must be careful about investing too much in these pieces. Pine and oak pieces left outdoors, especially those found in rural Canada to the north of us, can age beautifully in a relatively short time with this exposure. How many of these pieces have been accepted as seventeenth century will never be known, but one would best seek documentation before purchasing this kind of furniture. The squared leg and multiboard construction of nineteenth-century Canadian furniture is almost identical to our Pilgrim Period pieces. The search for this early furniture should be done through reputable dealers who have a record of handling the truly early pieces. To attempt to give any set clues for identification of differences would be hazardous. One must judge the age of the wood, and this requires personal examination of each piece. To judge by construction details would be mainly guesswork.

Excellent documentation is available for the Hadley chests that were made in Hatfield, Massachusetts, and Hatfield, Connecticut. Captain John Allis and Samuel Belding began a woodworking partnership about 1670, and there are records of these chests being made by the family until the 1720's. The original settlement was in Hadley, Massachusetts, but in 1690 the area on the west side of the Connecticut River was renamed Hatfield. Since they worked over such a long span, and turned out many marked works, they have gained in importance because their work is collectible.

While earlier work has been documented as having been done by Nicholas Disbrowe in Hartford and Phineas Pratt in Weymouth, Massachusetts, present-day collectors would find little chance of locating any of their work. On the other hand, Hadley chests, though rare, do change hands from time to time, generally at auction and estate settlements. The earliest of these chests was no more than a box that rested directly on the floor. Although glue was used by the Egyptians as far back as 1500 B.C., the dovetailing of the sideboards was used to make a strong chest that would not be subject to warping or twisting or loosening of glue. Secret compartments were installed for valuables, as well as iron locks. Often, these would be concealed with a movable piece of carving. A continuation of the stiles (the boards at each end) formed the first legs that went straight to the floor. These were later modified with cutouts in them for beautification. Then the Dutch style of ball or turnip feet was copied, and these remained with the chests well into the eighteenth century, until the Chippendale Period.

The tall chest evolved from the Hadley chest as longer legs were added to raise the box from the floor to make it easier to use. Then a drawer was added beneath it for greater storage space, and then another separate chest of four or five drawers was made to rest atop the base. These chests-on-frames remained popular until after the turn of the century, when Dutch cabinetmakers again thought it unnecessary to waste space with long legs. They extended the drawers to the top of a legged frame that held them barely above the floor.

Carved Hadley chest, Connecticut Valley, seventeenth century. *Bennington Museum, Bennington, Vermont.*

Some of the late seventeenth-century chests were called "marriage chests," and were used as a girl would use her hope chest today. Often these were decorated with paintings and ornaments, and sometimes they were gilded. The idea of the chests came from the old country, which must also have often prompted the painting. This beautification, a form of folk art highly appreciated today, adds to the value.

Bible boxes are another well-preserved product of this period. These were made to rest on a table, or Bible stand, and were elaborately carved in oak. Most had locks—some say to protect the Bible from thieves. Others feel that valuables were stored in the box along with the Bible, since it was felt that no thief would desecrate one of the boxes for fear of spiritual retaliation. Reverence must have been shown them, since many have survived this era. They were made in abundance during the eighteenth century, then seemed to go out of favor.

At the turn of the century, furniture making was a going business in the seaport cities. There was a growing demand for housewrights to construct new homes for successful tradesmen, and for talented carvers to embellish the designs in a manner we marvel at today.

Woodcarvers really came into their own at this time. The fairly large William and Mary furniture was still in vogue in this country until about 1720. This was the rather heavily styled furniture with many legs, and stretchers to support them. Native craftsmen made the furniture from oak, the most popular wood at the time, but many have turned up in walnut, maple, and even pine. Many pieces were veneered with highly figured walnut or maple burl, which was sheared from huge knots or from the root area of the trees. A good craftsman would take many thin layers from the same wood and match the grains on the drawers perfectly, so the piece would be in balance. In later periods crotched mahogany was done in this manner—by shearing a tree at the junction of a large limb with the trunk, and by perfectly matching the wood thus obtained on each side of the drawers. The William and Mary Period was not without beauty, and many graceful pieces were made—court cupboards, similar to a type of buffet server for the dining room; and press cupboards, which were low chests of drawers with the highboys on legs, objects that were both impressive and architecturally correct.

Chairs were made in a rather rigid fashion, with straight backs and legs; but the upholstering was comfortable, and interesting turnings added to their basic beauty.

William and Mary turnip-foot chest, Massachusetts, circa 1700. Original tear-drop pulls and brasses. *Courtesy Lion d'Or Antiques, Manchester, New Hampshire.*

Fine William and Mary painted chest, circa 1700, with trumpet turnings. *Shelburne Museum, Inc.*

A room at Dutton House, showing a fine painted William and Mary chest, gateleg and side table. *Shelburne Museum, Inc.*

Early maple gateleg table, circa 1700–1720, Massachusetts, with vase and ring turnings. *Courtesy E. L. Davis.*

On the whole, the period produced rather large furniture, and little of it survived in New England. Only museums appear to be stocked with display pieces. If a buyer decides to stock a supply of furniture of this period, he embarks on a rather perilous venture. Not much is available, and determining authenticity is a problem. One is likely to find English imports of more recent vintage, done in the manner of the old. Because a style went out of fashion does not mean production of it stopped; perhaps only less was made. We are fairly certain that there was much manufacture of furniture of this style in oak during the last century. A hundred years can age wood very nicely, and kicks and bruises during this time can make it appear quite authentic.

A product of this period that has survived in quantity is the gateleg table. Most authorities believe this design originated in England, and found its way here quickly. It was the answer to the problem of a small house where floor space was at a premium, and it caught the fancy of cabinetmakers and homeowners alike. Since a table is functional, and would be kept in usable condition, many have survived. Most were in oak, but pine was popular in the country areas. In addition, some were made of what is called Spanish pine, imported from the Caribbean. This would look more like our native southern yellow pine than like the New England white pine. Because walnut and mahogany came into their own during this period, it is not impossible to find an old gateleg made in these woods.

Always check the tops of these tables to make sure they are original. Replacement of tabletops in antique furniture is second only to the repair of legs and bases on chests. Quite often the large boards would warp or split and be replaced. Because they were hinged, it was easy to become careless and rip them off their hinges. Tabletops often were liable to burns from lamps, candles, or hot cooking pots. A top repaired even as recently as fifty years ago can be difficult to tell from an old one. If pegging was used to join the top to the base, this could easily have been done again in the same manner, and aging would hide the evidence of the work. (Perhaps the answer is that if you have become expert in the examination of antiques and can't tell, neither is anyone else likely to.) Gateleg tables seem to have disappeared when the Queen Anne styling came in, not to return until the Victorian Period in the middle of the nineteenth century. They are still being made today.

There are ways to identify English and American pieces. Abroad, they had exhausted the supply of large trees, and had to work with smaller boards. Check drawer bottoms. American makers would chisel out one large plank and run it from side to side, the whole length of the drawer, chamfering it so it would fit into the sides of the drawer. English craftsmen generally used two or three boards in a drawer bottom and ran them from front to rear or in the direction of the width of the drawer. Furthermore, our drawer bottoms were invariably of pine; the English would have used deal, oak, or possibly elm.

In addition, the English, trying to refine their techniques, began to do away with pegging the joints where two pieces of wood came together under stress. Examine where stretchers join the legs of chairs and where frames of tables join the legs. The Americans pegged throughout the Hepplewhite Period at the end of the eighteenth century, but pegging in English pieces almost totally disappeared in the Queen Anne Period in the early part of the century.

In any case, consider wisely before investing in furniture of the William and Mary Period in New England. Most of what you locate will be English, and worth less than American-made pieces, and most will not be of the 1700 vintage. When buying pieces as old and as

Delicate oval-top maple Queen Anne table, with Dutch foot. Rhode Island, circa 1710–1720. *Courtesy E. L. Davis.*

important as this, be sure to insist on a written guarantee as to age and the area of manufacture.

Queen Anne ascended the throne in 1702. She is said to have been a frail girl, not in good health. Reputedly, the cabinetmakers changed their designs as a tribute to the fragility of their new monarch, and thus evolved a period of true refinement in the art of woodworking. Gone were the heavy underpinnings of chairs and tall chests. They were replaced with clean-lined rounded forms in legs, chairbacks, and chest tops. Ornamentation was at a minimum—the beauty of the pieces lay in their pleasing proportions and delicate look. Though the queen died in 1714, the style named after her continued until the middle of the century. While some say we were not influenced by this period until about 1720, there is evidence to the contrary. The work of New England craftsmen at that time was about on a par with English work.

The Boston area now had many fine workmen. Even though a trip from England took up to a couple of months, there is evidence that the colonies kept abreast of the news from home, including the latest styles. The curved cabriole leg and the pad foot or duckfoot, along with variations like the Spanish toe and drakefoot, replaced the old trumpet turnings and heavy ball feet. The "tallboys," as they were called in England, suddenly appeared with rounded bonnet and broken arch tops to replace the earlier flat tops. Many of the country Queen Anne highboys were made in New England with flat tops, but city cabinetmakers favored the fancier construction.

Most of the English tall chests of this period were made of walnut and mahogany. In the 1720's walnut grew scarce in France and Virginia, and what was available was of poor quality. The rapidly expanding merchant trade with the Orient and the Caribbean made shipments of mahogany possible, and it became the favored wood here. If a piece of furniture is made of maple, birch, cherry, or pine, it almost has to be American. It it is walnut, oak, or mahogany, workmanship is the key, and the construction must be examined. Always check the drawer bottoms first.

This period produced the chest-on-frame, the chest-on-chest on a frame, and the chest-on-chest. They are exactly as described. The idea of building a separate frame on which to rest a chest might have come about as the result of damage to the fragile frames when they were moved about within a house or carried over rough roads. Maybe the

Graduated drawer maple chest in perfect proportions, 36 inches by 58 inches; bandy-leg in Queen Anne Style. Goffstown, New Hampshire, circa 1750.

Fine Queen Anne tiger maple desk on frame. Vermont, circa 1720. *Photograph by Stephen Greene.*

idea was that if such damage occurred, a new, legged frame section could be built easily, without sacrificing the quality of the chest. When purchasing a chest-on-frame, you should examine the frame carefully to make sure it is not a new one. Chest tops from this and the later Chippendale Period have often been placed on new frames to make up functional pieces, and because it was not unusual for bottom sections to become separated from top section, legs and frame would be added. Any chest with four drawers of either period should be examined closely, especially if the drawers are graduated in size. Five- and six-drawer top sections were rarely made, so when you find a graduated chest with five or six drawers, the chances are less likely the base is new, because it was probably made that way to begin with. Nevertheless, these still should be checked, as the Queen Anne legs are fragile, and much could happen to them over the span of 250 years.

The chairs of this period gradually lost their stretchers, and the vase-and-ring and sausage-turned legs of the previous designers gave way to the arched cabriole leg with designs of delicate feet. The Gothic and Tudor look of the carvings, which emphasized heavily cut panels and raised split spindles, were replaced by the more graceful fan, shell, inverted S and molding cutouts. Massive chests narrowed in width to a pleasing 34 or 36 inches, and slant-top desks that came originally on frames had lower drawers added to create beautiful and functional pieces. Some English and Dutch pieces of furniture evolved in the middle of this period with a sort of bracket foot that was restyled and improved by Chippendale in later years. Because the American pieces generally did not use this foot until these later years, any furniture that has Queen Anne characteristics and not the cabriole leg must be examined for possible foreign manufacture.

There are exceptions, however. There has been an exchange of opinions by experts on such furniture as the secretary-desk that is at the Warner House in Portsmouth, New Hampshire. The pictures on pages 24–25 show why antiquarians have traveled many miles to see it. It stands seven feet high, and is made of a combination of walnut and walnut veneer on secondary wood. The double arched design at the top with mirrored doors and carved gilded finials of cherubs and mother with child definitely give it a European look. Behind the doors are thirteen drawers; some suggest these represent our original thirteen colonies. As the lid comes down, the secretary section in the lower case pulls out,

◀
At the Warner House, Portsmouth, New Hampshire, is America's most interesting piece of furniture. Differing opinions concerning country of origin, age, and maker have aroused great interest in it.

Open doors reveal interesting thirteen-drawer arrangement, which some suggest symbolizes the original colonies.

▶
The top dummy drawer of the base lowers to form a secretary section, which may be pulled out.

▲
Carved figures whose bases do not match the plinths on which they rest. *Photographs by the author, courtesy Warner House Association.*

an unusual addition to a chest of this type. The bracket base would suggest Chippendale design, but there is evidence that it was made before this period, in the early part of the eighteenth century. The carved figures may have been added at a later date, as they do not fit their plinths very well. This type of figured finial did appear on some Salem, Massachusetts, pieces and this has aroused speculation that the famous woodcarver Samuel McIntire might have had a hand in its construction, which would place it late in the century. Opinion is still divided as to its country of origin, period of manufacture, and age. The walnut interior would suggest English origin, but the pine drawer interiors contradict this. This chest is an exception to the rule that experts usually can quickly identify furniture, and suggests caution in buying pieces of such age and importance.

All periods overlapped each other in details of construction, and many items contain features of an outgoing period as well as an incoming period. These are referred to as "transitional" pieces. A great many articles reflect the transition from the period of William and Mary to that of Queen Anne.

The popular Queen Anne design had as a favored feature the short cabriole or bandy leg with a Dutch, or duck, foot. This was used in New Hampshire as late as the 1790's. Note the elegant Dunlap furniture documented as of that time. Naturally, cabinetmakers also used the more ornate Chinese-influenced Chippendale design to a great extent, as well as the plainer "country" Chippendale designs that evolved from his later efforts. But the Queen Anne legs and bases were used throughout the entire century. The fan carvings that were popular in the early 1700's were still much in evidence at the end of the century, too. The first Chippendale styling evolved from many influences: Chinese, Dutch, and French, and after a period of rather plain, delicate furniture, we entered one of highly carved and heavily ornamented pieces. Thomas Chippendale did not rely on inlay or veneer of his furniture designs to beautify them—the intricate hand carving was his decorative mark. The ball-and-claw foot, utilizing the same cabriole leg as the preceding period, was introduced. Later, Chippendale used the plain square leg, often fluted, for his chairs and tables, and created the familiar bracket base for his chests. In some pieces, this was no more than a continuation of the side and front boards at the corners, descending to the floor gracefully, with cutout skirts on front and sides.

Chippendale chest-on-chest, country style, from Acton, Maine. Maple with hand-cut brasses, bracket base. Circa 1760.

Early-nineteenth-century New England Chippendale chair. All is original. *Property of Holyoke Museum, Holyoke, Massachusetts.*

His chairs are unmistakable in style. Side chairs were marked with "ears," where the side posts joined the back, and often these served as a focal point for interesting carving. His ladder backs with ribbon and other design cutouts are regarded by many as the height of artistry in wood. His design book published in 1754 reveals that he made cases for tall clocks and mantel clocks—though no documented ones have been found.

Though not credited with a period design of furniture, the Adam brothers, Robert and James, greatly influenced cabinetmakers with their furniture styled in Greek and Roman designs. They were contemporaries of Chippendale, and some feel they influenced his work. Originally, they were architects, and they took up furniture design at the request of their wealthy patrons. They did not make furniture themselves; they hired competent craftsmen to do the work. They were responsible for the introduction of satinwood for inlaying and veneering. This was imported from the East Indies, and found such favor that all later designers continued to use it. It is interesting to note that they were responsible for the first fluted leg design, generally attributed to Sheraton, who came two periods later. Much of their work was painted or japanned, in keeping with the elegance of the times, and many present-day collectors wonder whether to refinish pieces that show the ravages of time by cleaning them down to the natural beauty of grained woods or by repainting them. Cabinetmakers did not seem to be influenced by the Adams' designs, as none in this style made by native workers has turned up—yet they influenced future designers whose works were copied in the United States.

Another little-known designer was Thomas Shearer, who published a book on styles in 1788 entitled *The Cabinet Maker's London Book of Prices and Designs*. He must have had a great influence on Hepplewhite and Sheraton, who worked during this time, as he is credited with designing the square tapered leg, attributed to Hepplewhite, and also used at first by Sheraton. He is responsible for the first sideboard as we know it today, and also designed innovations such as folding beds and beds that would unfold out of cabinets that looked like a chest of drawers. Certainly he influenced cabinetwork in this country, though George Hepplewhite probably receives most of the credit. (Hepplewhite's name became of sufficient importance to attach to the period following the Revolutionary War.)

As after most great upheavals, a period of austerity arrived after the Revolutionary War. The simple straight-lined designs of Hepplewhite had great appeal. He liked circles, which he used often in the design of his tables; shields, which are a characteristic of his side chairs, done in simple styling and in proportions that were easily worked with the primitive tools of the time. In examining possible Hepplewhite side chairs, one can check to see if they follow his original specifications and design: seat front 20 inches wide, 17 inches deep; height of seat from floor 17 inches; and height of back 37 inches. These proportions, fairly well copied in New England, may serve as a guide to exactly what you should look for in a Hepplewhite chair. Furthermore, he (and Sheraton who followed) used horsehair coverings extensively on sitting-room pieces. Quite often, these would be attached with gold- or brass-colored upholstery nails. Rarely does one see any pieces of this period in this fabric; horsehair is accepted generally as a product of the later Empire and Victorian periods.

The Hepplewhite Period produced many fine tables that still appear in shops and auctions quite frequently. Among these are the tilt-top game tables, some round and some square. Perhaps his greatest contri-

Card table, mahogany, American Hepplewhite. The design and carving are attributed to Samuel McIntire (1757–1811) of Salem, Massachusetts. It was undoubtedly made for Elias Hasket Derby in 1795. It has spade feet cast in ebony.

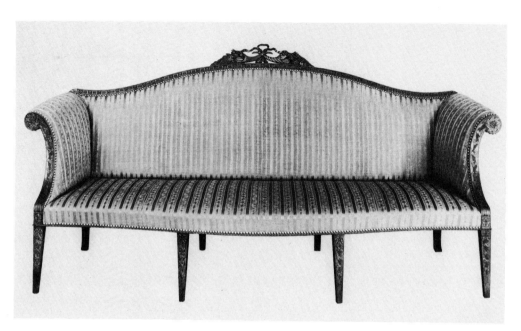

Mahogany sofa, American Hepplewhite, circa 1795. The carving is attributed to Samuel McIntire of Salem, Massachusetts. *Karolik Collection, Museum of Fine Arts, Boston.*

One of a set of ten carved chairs by Samuel McIntire of Salem, Massachusetts. Early nineteenth century. *Courtesy John Felsen, Henniker, New Hampshire.*

Hepplewhite tilt-top game table, maple, with maple and mahogany veneered drawer. New Hampshire, circa 1780.

Bowfront Hepplewhite graduated drawer chest; tiger maple and mahogany veneer, cherry top and sides. The brasses with lion design and casters on the feet are original. New Hampshire, circa 1790. The bowl is Chinese five-color porcelain, circa 1750.

bution in style, and something quite original, is his banquet table, which is unusual in that the basic table is made in two sections, rounded at the ends, with huge leaves dropping from the inner section of the table almost to the floor. Either one or both leaves can be raised to lengthen the table. A center section made as a regular dropleaf could be used in between these two sections to lengthen the table to accommodate a large gathering. All these were made with tapered legs. If you see one with fluted legs, it would have been made later in the Sheraton Period, and one with rope legs would be assigned to the Empire Period. These are the three periods when this banquet-table design was used. Examples from any of these periods are scarce, but very desirable.

Though Thomas Sheraton published his drawings as early as 1791, in London, their influence in the United States was not felt until the turn of the century, which marked a return to ornamentation through fluting and carving, and brought about some of the most graceful pieces available today. Sheraton furniture is still abundant in New England, and more and more collectors are turning to these relatively less-expensive pieces for decorative and functional use. This era marks what some consider the end of the Golden Era of furniture, since it is the last of

Bowfront transitional chest, Hepplewhite-Sheraton. Cherry, with maple and mahogany inlays. New Hampshire, circa 1800–1810.

Sheraton fluted-leg worktable in cherry and tiger maple, with satinwood veneered drawer. Maine, circa 1820.

Eighteenth-century Sheraton-type settee with original seat. From the Rand Homestead on Back Street, now Homestead Avenue, Holyoke. All is original. *Property of Holyoke Museum, Holyoke, Massachusetts.*

the all-handmade furniture. It was also the last of the truly light furniture. The following periods contributed much that was heavy and clumsy-looking.

Sheraton leaned heavily on inlay and veneer for beautification, and all the known woods, like satinwood, mahogany, rosewood, tulip wood, and others, were utilized to brighten his pieces. New England craftsmen carried on this tradition by utilizing the highly figured maples that dramatically set apart our furniture from the English, and resulted in pieces of such beauty that they command a great deal more in price than the imports.

An interesting feature of Sheraton-styled chests is that the perfect ones are just as wide as they are high. Thus it is easy to determine whether the legs have been cut down at any time.

During the Sheraton Period, because New England was being increasingly settled by inhabitants who were moving out into former Indian areas and who had to furnish their homes, more cabinetmakers were needed, and a wide range of furniture was created. Since many people still are living with the furniture made for or by their ancestors, such pieces are gradually finding their way to the marketplace. The country auction in New England is bound to offer Sheraton furniture, even if the earlier periods are not represented.

New England country furniture has come into its own. Only a few years ago, buyers were paying premium prices for highly decorated city pieces. Now the quiet quality of the more simply designed furniture is offering serious competition. The most highly desired, and thus the most expensive, combination of woods is that of cherry and tiger maple. Numerous pieces, such as small worktables, tilt-top game tables and chests, were done in these two woods, and those that appear for sale skyrocket in price. Next in demand are solid tiger maple; solid cherry; cherry and bird's-eye maple; solid bird's-eye maple; mahogany and maple; solid plain maple; solid birch, which is very often mistaken for solid maple; and pine. Very little walnut or oak furniture was made between 1720 and 1830 in New England. It is best not to look for it, since the pieces you will find most likely are from New York State, Pennsylvania, or the mid-South.

For some time there has been a move by historians to group the Sheraton and Hepplewhite periods into one designation as the Federal

Period. Perhaps there is some feeling that American craftsmen, though they worked in the basic designs of the English, at a time when the two countries were in and out of wars with each other, did manage to interject their own feeling into the work they did, to differentiate it from their overseas counterparts. Be that as it may, the term "Federal" is very much in keeping with the identification of our furniture made between 1775 and 1830.

Empire Period furniture is peculiar because of the great range of quality—there are many examples of excellent design and workmanship, as well as some of the most grotesquely designed and awkward furniture ever produced. One cannot label this period as desirable or not desirable. Unlike the periods that preceded it, where all the pieces were generally of good design, this era produced some monstrosities.

We do know that the Empire type of classic design originated in England about 1810, during the Sheraton Period, when finely reeded legs and delicate inlays were the rule. There were buyers who wanted embellishment in a grander manner, and designers outdid each other to supply the demand. Empire design came to the United States about 1820, and was mass-produced after 1830, when machine power tools

Finely styled Empire chair with fiddle-back, in mahogany and rosewood. Circa 1835. *Courtesy of E. L. Davis.*

came into being. Perhaps the artisans, with their new power tools, found that they could express themselves more easily in shapes and carvings that would have been laborious if done by hand. The acanthus leaf and lyre were worked to death by the finer cabinetmakers, and the country pieces with the elephant-trunk foot design, made later, robbed the period of greatness.

Despite the advent of power tools, there were many cabinetmakers in the country who still worked entirely with hand tools during this period; and it is confusing to see this style done both in all machine work and in all handwork. Because the basic requirement of an antique is that it be wholly or partially handmade, this distinction is very important in judging the Empire Period.

Duncan Phyfe, who learned the trade in Albany, New York, and later opened his shop in New York City about 1792, became one of the finest exponents of the classic style that was adopted primarily from the French Directoire and French Empire influences. His earlier graceful pieces were in sharp contrast to the later bulky designs he turned out at the time of his retirement in 1847. He is generally credited with the innovation of the pedestal-type of four-legged design that bears his name, but

Fine Sheraton-Empire bowfront chest in mahogany with satinwood plume veneer. *Chase House, Strawberry Banke, Portsmouth, New Hampshire.*

this seems to be a style in use by many at that time. His finer early hand-carved pieces are on display in museums, and represent the finest design at that time.

John Henry Belter of New York, who worked from the middle 1840's to the middle 1850's, was an influential designer, well represented in museums as an example of the fine craftsmen at that time. His earlier pieces had the stamp of the Empire Period, but he later changed his design to that of the incoming Victorian Period, and succeeded in turning out what might seem to some works of art and to others highly carved monstrosities. This is a very provocative period, running the gamut from the very good in design to the very questionable. In the end, collecting is a matter of taste.

Most of our early New England homes are too small for the heavy pieces Belter and others made. They are finding much more favor in the antebellum homes of the South, which, because of their high ceilings, must have larger pieces that will be in proportion to the rooms, where they have a much better look than they do in the North, where they are out of proportion in a smaller room and take up needed floor space. As a result, the Empire pieces, unless of unusually early fine quality and handmade, sell for very little here. They are bought for their functional value rather than antique value, and are treated simply as usable pieces of furniture.

Though small drawers at the top rear did appear on some Sheraton pieces, the overhanging top drawer was a product of the Empire Period. Actually, such drawers spoiled the look of the piece and in many instances have been removed with the dowel holes left in the top filled with plastic wood or putty. Wooden knobs are appropriate, but many will be found with original brasses, and, if you're lucky, with the milky-glass Sandwich pulls. For years these chests went unnoticed unless some dealer bought them for the drawer pulls or handmade drawers that could be used to make up another chest in a different style. Many Empire pieces were made over by utilizing the handmade construction in them, which is the first thing an expert will look for.

With the growing shortage in furniture of the pre-1830 period, the graceful Empire pieces are coming into their own. The bulkier ones are still almost worthless, for age has done nothing to affect their original bad design—further proof that age alone does not make an antique. Taste, design, and construction count. Because most of the Empire pieces did not fill these requirements, there is a resistance to them.

Empire mahogany chest with crotched graining, champfered rope-carved legs, and scroll back. Circa 1840. *Bennington Museum, Bennington, Vermont.*

Typical pine chair, or hutch table. Mid-nineteenth century, New Hampshire.

The Victorian Period is as puzzling as the Empire Period that preceded it. Even though most of the furniture was machine made, there is much to be said for the fine styling of many Victorian pieces. Yet the majority would not be given house room in New England. The pieces are too heavy-looking, and some are rather grotesquely styled. The colonial home does not lend itself to the massive beds and chests, and the huge dining-room sets would swamp most houses fortunate enough to have a separate dining room. As a result, much of it has found its way to town dumps and fireplaces. That which is good is scarce, and prices are going up. What remains is now sent south by the vanload, where it is well received.

Back in the early days of this century, there was much importing of antiques from the Maritime Provinces of Canada. They would be shipped to Boston by boxcar, and unloaded onto horse-drawn wagons. The import dealers would often sell the pieces right out of the boxcar to waiting crowds who would have been told of the event in advance. There was Victorian furniture that had been made in England, and it found great favor with the Bostonians who had large town houses.

Little or no furniture of this period was made in New England. Most of it came from Michigan and the South, where huge furniture factories had been placed near the source of good supplies of wood. Chairs and much of the lighter furniture were manufactured in maple and birch.

Perhaps the greatest amount of construction was of what we refer to as "cottage furniture." We have all seen the pine bedroom sets, drop-leaf tables, and cane-seated chairs of this period that extended well into this century. Pine was a native wood, easily worked, and New England factories at that time worked more with it than with the hardwoods. Pine is well accepted by newcomers to antiques, and is a good investment in warmth and comfort as well as money. Most pine pieces are much cheaper than even the new inexpensive furniture of today, yet they are antique in look, are built much more strongly, and will increase in value as they grow older. Young marrieds are wisely seeking out these pieces and either refinishing them or painting and decorating them.

The best pine pieces, such as chests, lift-top commodes, and tables, should be of single-board construction, where one wide pine board makes up the end, top, or surface. If more than one board is used to make up a top, side, or table leaf, it has considerably less value. Among chests, those with round corners at the front are most valuable. Size is important; the smaller ones are worth more.

The best lift-top commodes are those with solid plank sides, round corners, a single door, and a single drawer in front. Pine chests with mirror wells, or with added small drawers on top at the rear, are less valuable. Cane-seated chairs are still relatively inexpensive, but be advised that having them re-caned can be costly. Not too many years ago, re-caning would be priced according to the number of holes that were pierced around the seat to receive the cane. An average figure was seven cents a hole, which would keep the price under five dollars (the average chair had seventy holes). Check the prices of local re-caners before you buy, or perhaps you may want to do it yourself. There are caning kits available that are not too difficult to use, and there is a fine company, in New Haven, Connecticut, that supplies them.

The pine blanket chests with the lift tops, to be good, should be of single-board construction. Those with dovetailed corners are the best, since they are older. The taller blanket chests that look like a chest of drawers, but with two or three dummy drawers and a lift top, are getting quite scarce. There was a time when these were relatively undesirable pieces because of their size, but today collectors have found they make excellent storage chests that take up little floor space. Those that sold for twenty-five dollars a few years ago are now into three figures. But they are still a good buy because they are very functional and will always be in demand.

Pine dropleaf tables are still in abundance at low cost—those with single-board leafs and tops, plus well-turned graceful legs, are the best. The little worktables, or lampstands as they are sometimes called, are rising in value because the demand for the hardwood ones exceeds the supply. It is permissible for the top board to be three-fourths of an inch thick on these, unlike the hardwood ones, which must be five-eighths of an inch thick or less.

Pine was used in the construction of many trunks, so if you can find a dome-topped one that has been covered with leather, don't hesitate to soak off the leather and refinish the wood beneath. Pine kitchen chairs (the plank seat is pine; the legs, backs, and spindles most often are made of some harder wood) can be found almost anywhere. The thumb-back, or rabbit-ear, chair that was very common a few years ago is now the darling of the collecting set. It is still within the means of a moderate budget. The Hitchcock chair, which was first made in Connecticut in the 1830's, is still relatively low-priced, considering its age and quality. It is possible to buy the old ones for less than the new reproductions that are being turned out at the site of the original factory, as well as by other manufacturers.

Also in the pine-seated chair category are the many types of Windsor chairs. Some of these date well back into the eighteenth century, but most that are available were made in the last century. The greater the number of spindles, the greater the value. Be sure the spindles come through the chair rounds at the back so they can be seen; otherwise they are a reproduction. The birdcage design, with the four squared holes at the top, is more desirable than the step-down type, which has a graduated backboard at the top, or the simple type with a simple bent round to receive the spindles. The Windsor rockers with the raised comb-back structure are highly sought. If you ever wish to own one, don't hesitate even at today's prices, because these will continue to rise in value. The age of most Windsors is judged by the splay of the legs; those with the wider splay have greater age. This type of chair has been reproduced in many forms, especially for municipal buildings and

Eighteenth-century New England arrowback Windsor armchair formerly in Miller's Inn, Holyoke, Massachusetts (1749–1832). All is original. *Property of Holyoke Museum, Holyoke, Massachusetts.*

churches, so examine them carefully if you want to be sure you're getting an old one.

Tall pine beds are still somewhat difficult to dispose of in New England. If they come as a complete bedroom set, they have value. Many fine painted ones are being sold alone, at auctions, for as little as ten dollars. Sometimes they have scenes painted on them by itinerant painters who traveled throughout the country. Quite often, the artist would be asked to paint scenes of the farm, barns, animals, and so on, on all pieces of the bedroom set. Such sets have more value because of their primitive artwork than as furniture.

The hardwoods used in making furniture of the Victorian Period were mostly mahogany, walnut, and rosewood. But if you place any extra value on solid woods, be sure you check the pieces you buy. Probably more than half of them are nothing more than pine or some other secondary wood to which a figured veneer has been applied. You can tell by lifting the end of a chest—one that is solid mahogany or walnut cannot be lifted easily unless the drawers are taken out. Another way to check for veneering is to pull open a drawer; the face of it will show along the top edge of the drawer where it has been joined to the wood

Seven-spindle birdcage Windsor chair with bamboo leg turnings, circa 1810.

under it. And of course veneering was not used in any area where there is carving. Carvings are important in determining value; the favorites are those of fruits and flowers.

Victorian settees confuse the novice. He cannot understand why the prices vary so. The differentiating details are simple: The smaller ones are better; the design of the back and carvings is important—those with the graceful mirror or oval backs are excellent; others done in good taste with grapes or roses are good—and the wood from the back must be extended down over the arms (those with upholstered arms are not as good); a serpentine design on the front, plus carvings, is the best type; legs should be the cabriole style, with graceful carved knee extending down to an appropriate foot in keeping with the rest of the design.

Prices are still down on good Victorian sofas. The best full-size one I have ever seen was sold at an auction in Maine in 1967 for seventy-five dollars, before a gallery of dealers from all over the country. Since those of the preceding periods are fast disappearing, it is inevitable that the graceful Victorian sofas will have to take their places even in the New England homes. By that time, the best ones will be gone.

This was the era of the marble top. Marble has been used for centuries in furniture manufacture, but all of it was hand cut. With the advent of power machinery, about 1830, cutting was simplified, and designers took advantage of it. White native marble is best; colored imported marbles are less in demand. If marble has been badly stained, it is almost impossible to get it out. Though it is not unusual to have pieces of marble polished to remove stains, chips, and marks, this is done at the sacrifice of the natural look of it. Furthermore, this is not an inexpensive procedure. New England marble is shipped south, where it brings higher prices. Small square, round, or oval tables are still selling for less than fifty dollars at auctions and in homes, and many of the less interesting ones for no more than ten.

Dealers are reluctant to acquire Victorian furniture because there is very little money to be made on it in New England; it is bulky and heavy; therefore more men are needed to move it; it takes up too much floor space in a shop, and unless it is sold immediately to a dealer for shipment south, it will often remain on the floor a long time because the local people do not want it and tourists cannot conveniently get it home. Most New England dealers buy with an eye to the tourist trade—items that are easily wrapped and can be carried off in the family car. But if you want Victorian, New England is the place to buy it. Bring a pickup truck or be prepared to pay the high expenses of crating and shipping it.

At the other end of the Victorian scale are the graceful chairs. Those with qualifications similar to those of sofas and settees are the ones most in favor. Because they are up in price in New England, don't expect any great bargains. Comfortable chairs of earlier periods were scarce to begin with, and those that do become available are so high in cost that New Englanders long ago settled for the later furniture. Many Victorian chairs came originally with horsehair seats, but much excellent work has been done in replacing these with needlepoint and petit point, which will enhance their value even though they are not the original covering. Most of these chairs are in excellent condition, since they were reserved for parlor use and were probably used only on Sundays or when the parson came to call.

During the height of the Victorian era, there were still craftsmen turning out furniture in the styles of earlier periods. Country journeymen, who could not afford the machines used in the industrialized areas, were still working with crude tools. They would use parts of old

Graceful Victorian armchair in mahogany, with tapestry upholstery. Circa 1870.

furniture that was damaged or unwanted, and incorporate them into articles of their own design. This has resulted in controversial pieces, so far as documenting age is concerned.

In addition, during this period city craftsmen in the Boston area at the time of the Centennial of 1876 turned out hundreds of pieces in the exact style, woods, and workmanship of a hundred years earlier, creating what is now known as Centennial furniture. These were completely hand-built pieces, so well made that unless you are familiar with them you can be deceived. Because most of them were made with a great deal of veneer and inlay to beautify them, they are really handsome, and fit quite well in the Colonial home. Sometimes old drawers from Sheraton or Empire pieces were incorporated within Centennial pieces, and since they were completely handmade and well aged, it is difficult to distinguish a Centennial from an authentic item. The best way to identify a Centennial chest, let us say, is to look at the boards on the back—quite often these are nothing more than sheared mahogany, and are not the hewn pine planks that would have been found in an old one. The interior construction can deceive you unless you look at the nails that were used to put it together; they differ from the square hand-cut ones that predated 1876. Furthermore, the brasses most often were not of the early handmade variety. Look, too, at the manner of construction where the drawer-bearing boards at the front join the plank sides—the authentic ones would be mortised into the sides for strength, whereas the boards in the Centennial pieces would be just butted to the sides, glued into position, and nailed from the inside to strengthen them. The Centennial pieces turned out in Philadelphia are exceptions, and these are very difficult to identify because the Philadelphia craftsmen of old did not mortise their drawer boards into the sides since they were more oriented to English manufacture. One of these Philadelphia Centennial blockfront chests turned up in New England not long ago, where it sold for five hundred dollars. It was later sold again, in Pennsylvania, for seventeen hundred dollars, indicating that the Centennials have arrived.

With the approach of our second Centennial, one wonders whether such an ambitious project might be undertaken by woodworkers today. There are many excellent craftsmen still working with fine woods, many of them the equal of the finest who turned out the pieces we prize today. A demand for Bi-centennial furniture would encourage many craftsmen to produce works to be collected in the future even as we collect antiques today.

Bamboo furniture was also produced during the Victorian Period. Bamboo has always been popular in this country (note the "bamboo" turnings on chair and table legs of the early 1800's). Complete bedroom sets were made of bamboo in thicknesses not ordinarily seen in this country. Because we are accustomed to seeing slender fishing poles or small bookcases with thicknesses of bamboo of no more than an inch used in their construction, it is surprising to see a bamboo bed with posts four inches or more in diameter, and supporting members not much smaller. I have never been able to find out if these were made in this country or abroad, but many were turning up almost twenty years ago. Today they have almost disappeared, as bamboo is very "in," and seemingly the more massive the pieces, the greater the value.

Some people like to refer to the Lincoln era as the American Home Period. At that time, many home-improvement items came on the market, such as iron cooking ranges for the kitchen, platform rockers, velvet upholstered furniture, tasseled drapes, highly decorated oil lamps, and the pine furniture that bore little resemblance to the massive Victorian pieces in hardwoods. Sleighback rockers are native to this period. They were designed for function and comfort, with little thought to the prevailing styles of other artifacts around them. During this period, when we were still crossing the threshold of the Industrial Revolution, and when people from the farms were moving to the city to be closer to the factories, many artifacts were designed strictly for urban use in tenements. Little thought was given to design, and as a result many of these pieces are difficult to attribute to any particular period. In essence, these are the American Home pieces.

The 1890's saw the advent of the mission-styled oak furniture that was dominant until well after World War I. The oak was rugged, most of it cut very square, which was simplest, and made to last forever. Until recently, these pieces had no appeal, but now the smaller ones—like commodes, porch rockers, hall trees, and round kitchen tables—are becoming more popular. Texas dealers acquire vanloads from New England, where there still are few buyers. Again, because this is heavy furniture, not easily carried off in an automobile, native dealers are wary about buying it. Machine made, without character or style from the standpoint of age, it is looked upon as durable, interesting furniture from the past that is cheaper than new, and very much at home in areas whose heritage may not go back much further than the 1890's. Mission styling derives from furniture of Spanish origin that was used in the early missions in the West and Southwest. Today, when mission pieces are shipped to Texas, they are going back to where they were most appreciated in the first place.

Through the twenties and thirties we were deluged with the walnut waterfall and blond oaks, and were introduced to the very sterile Danish modern. Cherry and walnut came back into their own for very expensive furniture, but the use of these woods is rapidly dying out because of their high cost and the difficulty of getting them. The quality of this wood is becoming poor, and cabinetmakers are looking to other materials. There is a great rise in interest in Mediterranean styles, which are best exemplified by Spanish and Italian designs. It is incomprehensible that anyone would want to preserve the walnut waterfall furniture for facturers are attempting to create machinery and materials that will future collectors, but it is hard to predict public taste. Today, manumake it possible to stamp out chests of drawers through instant molding of all the parts. They will never have to be polished, and they will be

Shaker rocker from the Enfield Colony, New Hampshire. *Shelburne Museum, Inc.*

impervious to household liquids. Perhaps this is the furniture of the future. Paper mills and furniture factories are consuming our forests so rapidly that it will be no surprise if both industries will be forced by law to turn to synthetics at some time in the not too distant future. If so, prices will continue to go up on antique furniture, which will be prized by those who will still want the warmth and beauty of wood.

Some of America's collectible early furniture was made by the Shakers, a communal sect, originally from England in the 1740's, who spread to this country during the 1770's. Many inventions of artifacts that are still usable today are credited to these clever and industrious people; they are reported to have made the first clothespins, circular saw, and washing machine. Some of the Shaker colonies raised and packaged herbs that were sent around the world. Their furniture was well made, inexpensive, and eagerly sought after. Much of it has survived. Collectors frequent country auctions to find Shaker work.

Hardly an old farmhouse can be sold without several Shaker ladderback chairs coming to light. Though Shakers made ladder backs in abundance, the origin of the style preceded them in the Chippendale Period. The Shaker version is a country version made most often in

Shaker apple sorter's chair and a child's rocker. Elders sat on the small chair, sorting apples, because it was close to floor. *Shaker Museum, Centerbury, New Hampshire.*

maple, birch, or hickory. The seats were splint, rush, or cane, and later a woven webbing was used. The numbering of the chairs at first took place at Mount Lebanon, New York (right in the heart of the Capital District), the first of the Shaker colonies. On the back of the top rung, you may find a number impressed or burned in—this would be like a catalog number that would identify the type of chair it was. These would be numbered 1, 2, 3, and so on. Most likely the numbered ones you might find would be the New York chairs. The finials atop the side posts can be a good clue to Shaker origin. Those with a mushroom, clothespin, or teardrop look may very well be theirs. The raised front legs are a good indication, and some of these had a mushroom-carved top. The number of ladders in the back or their shape is not a dependable clue, as this type of chair was made just about everywhere and in similar design.

When the bentwood chair came to this country in the latter part of the past century from the Scandinavian area, the Shakers turned out their own version. This has the woven web seat and back, all of which was done by the Sisters. These were most often made of hickory, which bent well under steaming, and held its shape. Though the chair has a rather modern look (from the viewpoint of antiquity), as with many items, age alone is not the most important consideration. I am sure that many of these bentwood Shaker chairs go unrecognized today and that people assume they have no historical importance. The best way to recognize them is to study examples at the existing Shaker colonies. The basic design and proportions should be studied at great length.

Many other types of furniture and useful household items were made by this sect, including cupboards, chests of drawers, candlestands, tables, boxes of all types, and smaller items such as clothesbrushes, stereoscope viewers, kitchen utensils, and the like.

The Shakers had salesmen on the road who were effective in spreading their wares all along the Eastern seaboard and as far West as Ohio. Several good books have been written on Shaker design, and I would recommend reading one before beginning to buy.

Interest runs high in Shaker artifacts because of their handworkmanship, design, and country quality. Since the sect has almost disappeared, collectors will have to be content with the supply at hand. Already the increased interest in this work has resulted in higher prices. But there is still time before all the old farmhouses are emptied.

Generally, the greater amount of handwork that goes into a piece, the greater the value. We like to see handwork utilizing different kinds and colors of wood, different grainings of wood and different embellishments such as inlay and veneer. Of interest to the collector is the work of wood-carvers who created decorative pieces by utilizing, in keeping with the decorative taste of their time, ideas drawn from Greek mythology and architecture. Pillars, columns, acanthus leaf, and faces of gods were widely used.

During the seventeenth century, carving took on new importance as better tools were being made and different woods were being imported from America and the Caribbean, as well as the Orient. The artisans on the Continent were far ahead of those in the British Isles until the Restoration, which began in 1660.

Charles II brought the Stuart dynasty back to the throne. He later married Catherine of Braganza, a Portuguese princess. She brought much furniture with her to England, and its highly carved design influenced cabinetmakers for many years. It was in keeping with much of the work being done on the Continent. England, up to this time, had very little trade with the Continent, but now was able to import

Eighteenth-century cherry slant-top desk, made in Norwich, Connecticut. Note the heavy leg construction, unlike northern New England designs. *Hammerslough Collection.*

Ball-and-claw-foot highboy of finely carved mahogany with flame finials. American, circa 1780. *Courtesy of Louis Joseph.*

Very rare Connecticut Valley porringer-top table, circa 1710–1720. *Hammerslough Collection.*

the finest in French and Italian furniture, along with ideas for making it themselves. Many of their wood-carvers learned their trade with the stone carvers in Italy. The French "Rococo" style was in vogue. This is a loose adaptation of the word *rocaille*, which literally meant "a pile of rocks."

Because wealthy persons in England began to import furniture, as well as have it made locally, it is difficult to tell the country of origin during this period. We know that most of it was carved in oak and walnut, but rosewood, mahogany, and teakwood also appear quite frequently. Evidently, this heavily carved furniture was not held in great esteem even then. It gave way to furniture in the William and Mary style, which was austere by comparison.

The big question today is what to do with these Restoration pieces when we find them. Authentic objects and their many reproductions keep turning up in homes and antique shops. Very few people can tell the old from the relatively new, and very few can place a proper value on them.

It would be very difficult for the novice to tell a hand-carved piece from one carved by machine during the Victorian Period when these fancy pieces came into vogue again. Most Victorian pieces are machine carved, which is one reason they are low in price compared to those turned out by hand before these machine tools came into being, about 1830. Yet those that can be authenticated as having been made in the seventeenth century bring very little more in price. Not many of the earlier pieces are found in perfect condition, as delicate carvings break off easily. Not everyone likes highly carved furniture—for instance, people who wish to have early American homes. It is difficult to find sets of these chairs. Most often they are one of a kind, and are very uncomfortable. Such highly carved chairs change hands at relatively low prices in New England.

There are areas in the country, like New Orleans and Mobile, where the culture was built on imported artifacts and where, years ago, it was much easier to have objects shipped from Europe than to have them come overland from the North. In addition, the many French and Spanish settlers in these areas preferred European stylings. For that reason, the highly carved pieces that bring low prices in the North would bring the top dollar in the South.

Special attention must be called to the work of John Seymour and his son Thomas in Boston; Benjamin Frothingham in Charlestown; the Townsend-Goddard families in Newport; and the Dunlap Circle, as it is known, in New Hampshire. These were all craftsmen of the highest order whose pieces will always remain the most sought after in New England furniture.

John Seymour came to Boston from Portland, Maine, in 1794, and shortly thereafter set up his cabinetmaking business. His son joined him in his work a little later, and continued it until 1842. Mahogany with satinwood veneer was their favorite combination, yet they worked in most woods fashionable at the time. Many of their glass-doored pieces had interiors that were painted blue, in much the same manner as the old Pennsylvania cupboards. "Sheer elegance" is the only phrase with which to describe their work.

The Townsend-Goddard families were joined by marriage in Newport, Rhode Island. Some of their finest work, including an impressive blockfront secretary and a labeled Townsend Hepplewhite banquet table, may be seen in the John Brown House in Providence. Four generations of this family worked from the time of the 1760's, but the greatest work seemed to be done right after the Revolutionary War. Their furniture is strikingly beautiful because of its proportions and craftsmanship. They are credited with being the originators of the block-front design, and also the only workmen who carved the undercut talons in the ball-and-claw foot.

Major Benjamin Frothingham served in the Revolution. He had been a cabinetmaker in his father's shop as early as the 1750's. After the war, he resumed his work in Charlestown and was one of the cabinetmakers who designed blockfronts. Because the bases to his chests and desks differ from those of the Newport craftsmen, it is at least possible to recognize one from the other. He used the serpentine design a great deal, and worked mostly in mahogany.

Less is known about the Dunlap Circle in New Hampshire. It is believed that this family group, which worked from about 1740 to 1830, was started by Samuel Dunlap II, who at first was a carpenter and joiner, and worked at building churches and paneling rooms. Major John Dunlap was another noted member, and he along with others helped create a style of furniture not duplicated by anyone else. While the city craftsmen would beautify their pieces with inlays and veneers, the Dunlaps concentrated on beautifying theirs with the grainings of solid woods. Their carved details, like dentil molding, stop fluting, inverted S, fishtail, and shell and fan, were so distinctive that attribution can be fairly certain when a piece has these characteristics. The Currier Gallery in Manchester and the New Hampshire Historical Society in Concord, as well as other major museums, feature their work.

As a matter of reference, the following is a list of some of the most highly regarded cabinetmakers who did their work during the handmade period of furniture prior to 1830:

Connecticut
    Hartford: Eliphalet Chapin, Lemuel Adams
    Norwich: Benjamin Burnham
    Old Saybrook: Charles Gillam
    East Windsor: Eliphalet Chapin
    Newtown and Southbury: Ebeneezer, Elijah, and Joel Booth
Rhode Island
    Newport: Goddard and Townsend families
    Providence: James Aborn, Matthew Egan, Thomas Howard, Jr.,
        Joseph Rawson, Charles Scott, Philip Potter, Judson Blake,
        and John Carlile
Massachusetts
    Boston: John and Thomas Seymour, the Skillins family, consisting of John, Samuel, Simeon, and Simeon, Jr.
    Charlestown: Benjamin Frothingham
    Salem: Samuel McIntire, William Hook, and Nathaniel Appleton
    Concord: Joseph Hosmer
    Ipswich: Thomas Dennis
    Dorchester: Stephen Badlam, Jr.
Vermont
    Salisbury: Ira Smith
    Coventry: William Weaver
New Hampshire
    Salisbury, Goffstown: the Dunlap Circle, including John, Samuel
        II, and many others
    Portsmouth: John Gaines, III, and Nathaniel Marshall
    Candia: John Lane
Maine
    Winthrop: Samuel Benjamin

CHAPTER 3

Glass

GLASS is perhaps the most popular of antiques. Indeed, bottle collecting is the third most popular hobby in the country, running very close to coins and stamps. Glass, so varied in design, so colorful and so widespread, is possibly the most fascinating area of antique collecting. New Englanders like to think they were first in the production of almost anything collectible, yet in the production of glass they were not. Early New England glass manufacturers operated within a limited local area, and often closed their doors once the available wood for the kilns and silicas was exhausted. It wasn't until 1818 that the New England Glass Company was founded in Cambridge, Massachusetts. It became the first large-scale manufacturer to survive for a long period of time—until 1888.

It is a great challenge to document glass, since designs were copied freely, workers were very transient, foreign glassblowers would emigrate here and turn out designs just as they had in Europe, and the quality of the glass was always similar, making attribution by age and color almost impossible. Yet there are certain small clues to permit today's student to calculate origin and age with a great deal of accuracy.

The first ambitious gesture toward creating a glassmaking facility in New England probably can be credited to Robert Hewes, a Bostonian who left home in 1780 during the Revolutionary War to set up business in Temple, New Hampshire. He hired deserting Hessian soldiers who were supposedly well versed in this field. Two fires eventually put him out of business. He attempted to make bottles and window glass, and should a piece of his work be found and documented, it would be considered a rarity indeed.

In 1787 Hewes returned to Boston and was instrumental in founding the Boston Crown Glass Company, which specialized in window glass. This venture, which expanded several times, finally ceased operations in the 1820's. But Hewes had excited the interest of local craftsmen, who eventually went on to form companies responsible for some of the finest glass turned out anywhere.

An offshoot of the Boston Crown Glass Company was a works set up in nearby Chelmsford. This was destroyed in 1829, rebuilt, and subsequently, because of the scarcity of fuel, moved to Suncook, New Hampshire. The Suncook venture ended in 1850. Bottles, as well as glass vases and bowls, were manufactured, much of it in the lime-green color. Very little of the Suncook glass can be found and documented, but what has been located is of good quality.

In 1814 the Boston Porcelain and Glass Company began in business in Cambridge and after several rather unprosperous years sold out to the now famous New England Glass Company. One of our most famous early glassmakers, Deming Jarves, was a member of this company. Under his guidance, the company prospered in the making of both art and utilitarian forms of glass, and he was responsible for the first stable glassmaking concern in New England. He introduced new manufacturing techniques in an effort to improve mechanized work and to make mass production a reality.

In 1825 Jarves purchased twenty thousand acres of woodland at Sandwich, Massachusetts, on Cape Cod, and opened the highly productive Boston and Sandwich Glass Works. Their goods were immediately successful, and the company became a serious competitor in the field. This concern is credited with being first in the mechanical pressing of glass, which they did as early as 1827. From then on, this pressed ware seemed to be the center of the firm's successful operation. As the company had its own docks and could load ships directly, Sandwich glass was sold throughout the world. And because of the company's large distribution facility in San Francisco, perhaps as much Sandwich glass can be found on the West Coast as on the East. Shipments came all the way around South America to satisfy this area's rapidly growing demands after the Gold Rush of 1849.

More glass has been attributed to the Sandwich Works than could possibly have been made there, and eager collectors regard this early work as among the most highly desired.

A case containing early blown candle-sticks and lamps, and lacy Sandwich dishes. All are from the Boston and Sandwich Glass Company, shortly after 1830. *Courtesy Sandwich Glass Museum.*

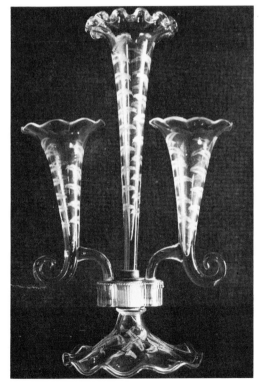

Epergne with typical Sandwich fern engraving, made in the 1870's. Note the glass holder for vases, which were always used in Sandwich pieces rather than a metal fitting. *Courtesy Sandwich Glass Museum.*

Early Sandwich candlesticks, with blown top joined by a glass wafer to a pressed base. Circa 1830–1835. *Courtesy Sandwich Glass Museum.*

Famous petal-and-loop candlesticks, pressed in two parts and joined by a wafer of glass. Because of this, they were often of two colors. Sandwich, 1840–1850. *Courtesy Sandwich Glass Museum.*

Madonna or "Draped Lady" candlestick on the left was made at Sandwich between 1840 and 1850, as were the two crucifix candlesticks. The Madonna candlestick on the right was made in the early 1900's, when factory was reopened for a short time. *Courtesy Sandwich Glass Museum.*

Deep ruby-red chalice made as a presentation piece at Sandwich. Much Bohemian-type glass was made at Sandwich by workers who came from Europe to work there. *Courtesy Sandwich Glass Museum.*

Windowpane with fragment dug up at
site of Boston and Sandwich Glass Company. Several pieces of this pattern are
to be found in Sandwich, used as side
panels on each side of front doors in
early homes. *Courtesy Ruther and Kenneth Wakefield.*

Rare lacy Sandwich glass with eagle motif on all pieces except the one at upper
right, which is Fort Pitt glass, Pennsylvania. *Bennington Museum, Bennington,
Vermont.*

While collectors are most familiar with the clear blown molded and pressed glass of the Sandwich Works, this concern was also responsible for some of the most beautiful work in colored glass and glass art forms known to the industry. A visit to the Sandwich Glass Museum near the original site on the Cape provides an education in a world of forms and designs that would not quickly be credited to the Sandwich Works except by students and historians who have done their homework. The concern closed in 1886 because of labor difficulties.

In 1837 Jarves formed the Mt. Washington Glass Works in South Boston for his son. Later, under new owners, it was moved to New Bedford, where in the 1890's it merged with the Pairpoint Manufacturing Company. Pairpoint was a well-established, highly regarded silver-making concern, and this marriage of the glass- and silver-making firms resulted in some of the greatest collectibles available today. This plant went out of business only recently, in 1958, yet collectors' interest in acquiring anything with the Pairpoint or Mt. Washington name attached to it has grown dramatically. Even in later years, a great deal of their work was still done by hand, and as a result their goods are highly collectible.

Cut-glass ice-cream dish, extremely thick and heavy. Pairpoint, early twentieth century.

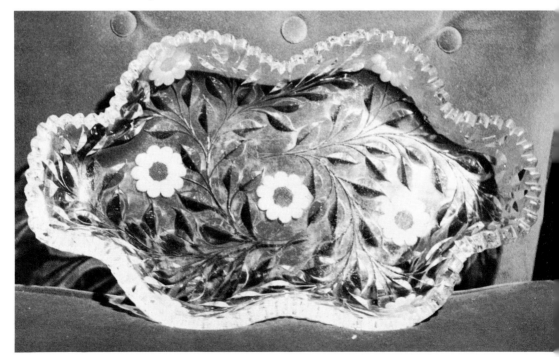

Rose amber vase, Mt. Washington-Pairpoint, with interesting folded collar, made in the 1890's.

(Left) Keene, New Hampshire, Masonic flask, and Keene sunburst, circa 1815–1820.

Connecticut contributed three early glassworks. One, the Pitkin Glass Works, was at East Hartford, and operated from the turn of the century to the 1830's. This concern gave its name to the now famous Pitkin Flask, whose form was widely imitated. The Coventry Glass Works and the West Willington Glass Works were organized during the War of 1812. The former lasted until 1848, and the latter until 1872. Both produced bottles, flasks, and related forms, and their work is highly sought after today.

New Hampshire also contributed several famous bottle-making and window-glass plants early in the nineteenth century. The New Hampshire Glass Factory was organized in 1815, in Keene, and lasted until 1856. It produced window glass, bottles, and utility and decorative pieces, mostly in the dark amber-green color.

Perhaps the more noted of the early Keene glassmakers was the Marlboro Street Works, opened by Henry Schoolcraft and Nathaniel Sprague in 1815. In 1817, after their business failed, it was taken over by Justus Perry, who operated it successfully until 1835. During this period, he turned out some of the most collectible flasks, including the famous Masonic and Sunburst flasks. He also turned out inkwells, candlesticks, and just about everything else needed by the homemaker of that day.

In 1842 Joseph Foster opened a glassworks in Stoddard, New Hampshire. This was later taken over by the Granite Glass Company. Also in and around this village were the New Granite Glass Works and the South Stoddard Glass Company, both formed in the middle of the century. Many of their pieces are well marked, and their flasks, inkwells, and candlesticks are among the ones most desired today. The dark amber-green color was the result of the natural silicas used. Because they used the eagle as a decorative motif a great deal, and with the eagle design so popular now, these flasks command top prices.

It is interesting to note that the lily-pad design was used here. Thought to have originated in New York State, the design actually started in New Jersey, and came by way of New York and Vermont to New Hampshire, where it was produced at Stoddard.

Attempting to attribute individual pieces to any of the three plants is hazardous unless the items are marked, because their work was so similar.

The Vermont Glass Works, the most noted in the state, was at

Salisbury, near Lake Dunmore. It was begun in 1812 by Henry School-craft, who later left to start the Marlboro Works in Keene. It closed in 1817 and reopened in 1838 under the name of The Lake Dunmore Glass Company. It operated until 1841, manufacturing bottles, window glass, and related items.

One of the least known and shortest-lived glassworks was the Port-land Glass Company, which operated in Portland, Maine, between 1863 and 1873. Much of its work is on display at the Portland Museum of Art in the Frank H. Swan Collection. The museum's brochure notes that the company's lamps, chimneys, and tableware won immediate success. They produced about fifty patterns, including their best known, the tree of life, as well as the Palmer prism, the frosted leaf, the loop and dart, the broken column, and the Portland banded in color. The coloring of Portland's maiden's-blush cranberry glass is unique, and is among the rarities in glass. Among the interesting pieces are those in the tree-of-life pattern that incorporate the name Davis, spelled out. This refers to Mr. W. O. Davis, the superintendent of the company. Though this company was late to manufacture pressed-glass pieces, its work was unexcelled.

Ewer in blown blue and clear glass, Portland, a very rare type. *Portland, Maine, Museum of Art.*

◀

Banded maiden's-blush cranberry Portland glass tumbler, circa 1853–1873. *Portland, Maine, Museum of Art.*

▼

◀

Three bowls of offhand production that probably originated at Lake Dunmore, Vermont, between 1813 and 1817. *Bennington Museum, Bennington, Vermont.*

Overshot design, Portland glass. This is very difficult to tell from crackle design. *Portland, Maine, Museum of Art.*

Portland glass night-and-day goblet, very rare. An owl is pictured, with a rooster on the opposite side. *Portland, Maine, Museum of Art.*

Frosted leaf, milk glass base oil lamp. Portland Glass. *Portland, Maine, Museum of Art.*

Portland glass ruby-stained dish in broken-column design. *Portland, Maine, Museum of Art.*

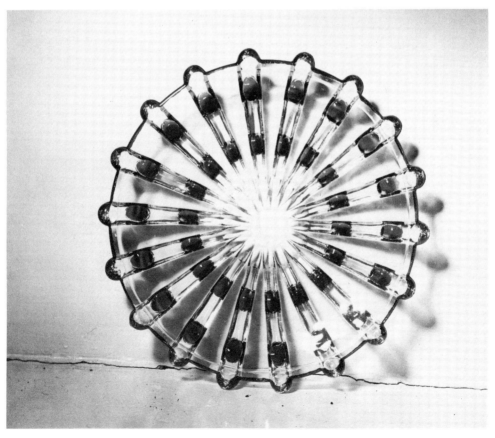

It is surprising how much glass from other areas came to New England. There is much from the Midwest, as well as from foreign countries. Despite the many New England factories, there was always a demand for non-native products. In Pittsburgh, around the middle of the nineteenth century, there were over 130 glass factories, all turning out large quantities of glassware. Their work was equal to that of the New England makers in the blown, molded, and pressed glass, but most collectors favor the New England pieces when it comes to the art-glass forms of the Victorian Period. This type of production reached its height in the 1880's when the New England Glass Company brought out Amberina, which was a process of shading amber into cranberry. This was accomplished by putting pure gold into the molten glass—the longer it was kept heated, the redder it got. The craftsman would start cooling the area that had turned amber from the heat, allowing the other half of the piece to turn as far as a deep cranberry color before cooling it. The Mt. Washington Glass Works quickly took up this process, but was found in violation of a patent. Under agreement, they continued to make it under the name Rose Amber, a term often applied to these pieces. The Amberina made at the Midwest plants was deeper in color than that made locally, and was called Ruby Amber Ware. The cased, or plated, pieces of this ware are very valuable. These were coated with an opalescent lining in the interior, which served to heighten the contrasting amber and cranberry colors on the outside.

Along came many other color combinations such as Peachblow (the white or light tinted blue graduating into a pinkish purple) and Wild Rose (a light tinted yellow shading into a light purple). Also popular is the Burmese, shaded from a pink to a yellow, and this was made only at the Mt. Washington Glass Works. In 1886 some of this was sent as a present to Queen Victoria, who liked it so much that she ordered more for Buckingham Palace. Later, an English concern was licensed to produce what was known as "Queen's Burmese."

Pomona glass, or Blue Cornflower, as some call it, was made at the New England Glass Works. This was trimmed with amber coloring and the blue cornflower design, and was made only for a very short time. A mother-of-pearl design in diamond pattern was made in New Bedford under the name of Pearl Satinware. This originated in Pennsylvania, but was quickly imitated in New England.

Other glasses made by most concerns were spatterware, which, as the name suggests, was made by rolling hot glass over small broken pieces of colored glass, and then forming it; spangled glass, which was made by rolling hot glass over bits of mica, either gold or silver in color, and which, after forming, was cased in with another layer of glass for protection; and Vasa Murrhina, which was made by rolling glass over real flakes of gold or silver. A Vasa Murrhina Company was established in Hartford, Connecticut, and the ware received its name from this concern, which made some of it. Agata ware, which is a mottled pink that sometimes shaded to rose or white, was made only by the New England Glass Company, and only for a couple of years. Thus it is extremely scarce.

It is not easy to find documentation for all these types of glasses, nor is it easy to learn to recognize each type. As for judging the nuances that differentiate one factory's work from another, there is a long road ahead. Many people have studied these glasses for years, and have found that many of these same types were also made abroad, adding to the confusion. Be careful, therefore, about proper attribution, and if you are paying a high price, be sure to get written documentation of type and origin.

Canary-yellow pressed tableware. Gothic arch covered sugar bowl. Peacock-eye plate. *Currier Gallery Collection, Manchester, New Hampshire. Photo by Finney.*

Blown-glass flytrap, which utilized vinegar, sugar, or honey. Its applied top would suggest 1830's to 1840's.

Easter canary-yellow pressed Comet (Horn of Plenty) butter dish with a Washington head finial. *Currier Gallery Collection, Manchester, New Hampshire. Photo by Finney.*

The early days of glassmaking saw many interesting shapes and sizes. The glassblower was an important man in the community, as he had a skill matched by few. The early works were mainly bottle and window glass, both made in much the same fashion. After a bottle was blown, the base of it would be attached while hot to a metal pontil rod, and then the top of the bottle was sheared from the blowpipe. From then on, the worker would mold the bottle to specification, and shape it carefully, returning it to the heat from time to time so it could be worked more easily. After acquiring the desired shape, the pontil rod would be broken off, leaving a rough, jagged spot, and the bottle would be set aside to cool. In the early days, little attention was given to the rough pontil mark, but in later years such marks would be smoothed so no one would get cut. The tops of the bottles were sheared off to receive a cork stopper. Because these were fragile, later on a reinforcing lip was attached while the bottle was hot, and this is called an applied top. After the idea of blowing into a mold was conceived, the workers had less to do. The two-part molds were carved from wood, and were called a snap-case mold. The bottle would still be taken from the mold on a pontil rod and handled with it until the top was sheared and finished properly.

Window glass was made by taking one of the large free-blown bubbles of glass and shearing it, making the hot glass lie flat. This would be held by a pontil rod while the shearing took place. The raised imperfections where the rod held the glass are called the "bull's-eye" panes of glass that adorn many doorways and doors in early homes.

Quite often, bottle molds would burn out after repeated use, with the hot glass taking its toll on the carved ridges inside. Though many companies had their names or initials carved into the molds, these sometimes wore off, making it more difficult to document the bottles. Some authorities feel that those that can be identified by design alone are worth more money because there were fewer of this type made.

Old unmarked bottles are perhaps the easiest old glass to identify, as the molds were individual to each concern. When the pressed-glass pieces came into being in 1827, blown by machine into metal molds, the chances of such identification diminished. Hundreds of different patterns were made and imitated by glass concerns everywhere. It was simple for one company to take a molded piece of glass and make a metal mold identical to it, and this is just what many companies did. So, again, be careful of attribution.

New England contributed two great glass-cutting concerns, the Mt. Washington Glass Works and the Union Glass Works that was founded in Somerville, Massachusetts, in 1854. These concerns rivaled the best work of foreign craftsmen, with the Mt. Washington Works turning out perhaps the heaviest and deepest cut glass known. Some concerns marked their cut glass by etching it faintly on one of the cut facets, usually at the bottom of the piece. To see this etching, hold it at an angle to the light.

Some heavily designed pieces often are called "near cut" glass. These are molded pieces done to resemble cut glass as much as possible. Cut glass is actually cut by holding it against a copper cutting wheel, and is work that demands the utmost patience and ability. Little wonder that a shortcut was sought—but without success. Cut glass was regarded as the ideal wedding present from the Gay Nineties right into this century, but fell out of favor until recently. Many people still have no regard for it, as it will mar a finished table or sideboard with its sharp edges. However, within the last ten years cut glass has begun to assume real value, and certainly it is among the collectibles. It brings much better prices in the South—most of New England's output going to Texas. New England is a good place to buy cut glass, but prices are considerably higher than they were a few years ago.

It isn't true that all glass that rings is good. Indeed, inexpensive glass purchased in a department store may ring. Originally, lead was used as a flux in the making of glass, and this would give the pieces weight and a good ring when struck. If a piece has other signs of age, you can be almost certain it was made before the 1860's. An employee of the New England Glass Company, Thomas Leighton, went to the Hobbs and Brocunier Company in Wheeling, West Virginia, and while there perfected the use of inexpensive lime as a flux for making glass. Out went the ring, and really good quality with it. The New England makers, striving more for quality, did not adopt this substitute, and as a result were not able to compete. Gradually, the New England concerns went out of business, while those in the Midwest survived.

The late 1800's also saw the arrival of iridescent glass, and Louis Comfort Tiffany helped pioneer the making of it. He had studied in Paris, and was intrigued with the metallic colorings on early Roman glass that had been dug from ruins. Iridescent glass had appeared as early as 1873 at an exposition in Vienna, but until Tiffany began to make it here, it was not really accepted in this country. Tiffany did not confine himself to glassmaking alone. He gained a reputation as an interior decorator as well as an innovator of designs for bronzes, lamps, and such items as desk sets. His famous Tiffany Curtain, which hangs in the Palace of Fine Arts in Mexico City, is his greatest achievement. It contains over two million pieces of glass fused together in a curtain large enough to hide the massive stage. His works are well marked; you will find the initials "L.C.T.," "Tiffany Studios," or the word "Favrile" stamped or etched on the bottom of anything of his. "Favrile" will be found on his colored glass pieces.

There was a time when Tiffany glass was not in general favor with the public. Many considered it gaudy compared with the works of such contemporaries as Lalique in Paris, Carder at Steuben in Corning, Durand in New Jersey, and Gunderson at the Mt. Washington-Pairpoint Works in New Bedford. The past decade has witnessed a renaissance of interest in their work, with a fantastic increase in the values placed on it.

Naturally, craftsmen of this type had imitators, and the first big one was the Imperial Glass Works in Bellaire, Ohio, a concern still in business today. In 1910 it began producing what we refer to as "carnival"

Carnival glass by Imperial Glass Co. and Northwood. *E. Ward Russell.*

New Imperial Glass souvenir nursery-
rhyme mug, in bluish iridescent glass.

Prophetic inscription on the basis of the
mug pictured above, made between the
Republican Convention and Election Day
1968. *Imperial Glass Co.*

or "taffeta" glass, and this was quickly imitated by many other works in that area. At first this glass was inexpensive and iridescent—eventually it was given away at fairs and carnivals as prizes and as premiums with the purchase of food. Refinements were not long in coming. Different colors were used, and many finely molded pieces were turned out. Much of the work was done by hand on the better pieces (it would take eight men about four or five minutes to turn out one item). The green- or purple-tinted bluish colors are quite pretty, and designs with fruits and birds are popular.

None of this glass was made in New England; it was all done in our Midwestern glass area around Pittsburgh, West Virginia, and Ohio. Much found its way to New England, where it now may be easily purchased. Those pieces with the Imperial cross mark and the underlined N in a circle, which came from Harry Northwood's plant in Newark, Ohio, are among the most desirable. Today, Imperial is still turning out much of this iridescent ware on order, but it has changed its bottom mark to an *IG*, to differentiate the old from the new.

The American Carnival Glass Association, numbering well over a thousand members (many from New England), has special commemorative pieces turned out each year. Already these have become collectors' items, as they are made in limited quantity, and the mold is then broken. The latest effort is the Nixon-Agnew elephant-handled mug (page 74), which, prophetically, was turned out between the time of the convention and election.

People have been collecting historical flasks and early blown bottles for a long time, but only within the past decade has this pastime grown into one of the greatest areas of collecting. Since there is a scarcity of the early bottles, people have broadened their tastes to include the newest. Companies now are turning out all sorts of bottles in both glass and china. Bottles are classified within different categories: figurals, medicinals, bitters, flasks, and historicals. The wide variety made since the beginning of the last century has resulted in collections that number in the thousands. People are digging old bottles out of refuse heaps behind farms, and quite often out of town dumps. All sorts of treasures are turning up. Some of these bottles have become quite pretty as a result of having absorbed minerals during their long burial, and color is a very important factor in collecting them. Many fine early flasks have risen into the three-figure bracket, and new prices are being set at bottle auctions as demand gradually exceeds supply.

Even in New England, documented eighteenth-century bottles are hard to find. Glassblowers were using the same blowing techniques well into the last century, and the newer glass could have been just as crude in look and color as the older. All the previously mentioned works turned out bottles, either blown or pressed, or both. Many are well marked, either with letterings or with identifiable designs. The early medicine men bought bottles to package their tonics and bitters, and liquor concerns helped spread some of our best bottles all over the country. Most companies had branches from coast to coast, and it is possible to find many prized eastern bottles out west.

In addition to bottles, glass collectors are turning to the glass insulators that are used on electric and telephone poles. The wide variety made, and the wide range of colors used, have sparked the interest. These and canning jars that date back to the middle of the last century are a new phase of collecting. Old-timers are shaking their heads and asking, "What will they collect next?" Canning jars and insulators are plentiful in New England. Cellars are still full of jars, even those with the desirable 1858 date on them. Along old long-abandoned railroad rights-of-way, one can find insulators that have been thrown away as workmen replaced them with new ones on utility poles that often paralleled the railroad.

New England is the home of the prized Keene, Stoddard, Pitkin, and Coventry flasks. Though prices for many of these are in three figures, they are a good investment. Those that were hand blown into molds, have their age documented, and have either a historical or political motif command the best prices. The dark olive-amber of the early pieces is perhaps the most desirable color, and the lighter-tinted aqua the least desirable. Flasks portraying George Washington, Lafayette, or other important historical figures are very important. Those with eagles, flags, or scenes of famous battles, like Bunker Hill, are good too. Some are quite unusual, such as the Keene and Coventry sunburst design, which is nothing more than simulated rays of the sun emanating from a central oval panel, or the Masonic flasks that picture an eagle on one side and Masonic emblems on the other. Railroad buffs vie in collecting Success to the Railroad flasks, as well as railroad-train bread platters. Grading these items as to worth is not practical, since their values change with each auction or bottle show. Bottle collectors' clubs and such publications as the *Antique Trader* keep collectors well informed on what is happening in the world of bottles.

Bottle collecting has taken on added importance as the search through attics, barns, and garages goes on for early bottles with their labels intact. They reveal much about early America and her medicine men. The bottles most easily found contained patent medicines. There were not many doctors, and almost everyone resorted to the panaceas and cures that were supposed to be in medicine bottles. Some of the claims made by their makers are astounding, and the labels make fascinating and humorous reading. The imagination of some of the copywriters would have earned them high-paying jobs on Madison Avenue today.

A fascinating collection of the medicinals of bygone eras is on display at the Apothecary Shop at the Shelburne Museum in Vermont. One can spend a day there just reading labels, marveling at the ingenuity of the early medicine men. A popular remedy must have been Dr. William's Pink Pills for Pale People—guaranteed to bring color and the flower of youth back to one's cheeks. Not to be outdone, a Dr. Wendell brought out his Ambition Pills, described as a great nerve tonic to fire one up on dull, dreary days.

If you planned to "tie one on" for the weekend, you could prepare with a Saturday Night Nerve, Brain and Muscle Tonic. A handy aid during an election year must have been Dr. Perrin's Voice Fumigator. This was guaranteed to do away with rumbling sounds in the heart, sounds of distant waterfalls, loss of voice, catarrh, and minister's throat.

Predating our United States Public Health Service by a hundred years was Dr. M. L. Byrne, who in 1864 marketed an Antidote from Tobacco. For guaranteed results there were Kickapoo Pills for Constipation. These were made by the Kickapoo Indians who settled in Ohio and struck up a thriving business in Indian witch-doctor medicines. They even printed catalogs, which are collectors' items today, listing a cure for every known ailment—and some that must have been invented.

An amazing development is the interest shown in new bottles. It is difficult to imagine a bottle made a few years ago commanding a price well into four figures, but such is the case, proving that age alone does not set the price on collectibles.

In 1953 the Jim Beam Distilling Company began packaging bourbon in specially designed bottles, some glass and some china. Since then, these have become very collectible, and people bargain for them all over the country. The company's peak was a special commemorative bottle put out in 1964 for the First National Bank in Chicago. One hundred of the blue-and-white decanters were made for the executives of the bank. The latest price at which one changed hands was $4,500!

Harold's Club in Reno ordered three hundred cases of bourbon packaged in bottles that looked like one-armed bandits. They expected to sell these in a year, but were completely cleaned out in ten days. Collectors drove to Nevada to be on hand when the boxcar was emptied, and ten thousand dollars' worth were sold in forty-eight hours. One out-of-state buyer bought fourteen cases for $1,400, and, to avoid violating any laws, spilled out the bourbon before departing.

The New Hampshire State Liquor Commission contracted for 14,400 cases of bourbon packaged in a china bottle shaped in the likeness of the state, with the head of the Old Man of the Mountain molded as the stopper. There was a frantic rush for them. Supposedly, after a long line had waited at the commission's main store in Concord, many people went away empty-handed, after others had been fortunate enough to get their limit of two. One lady was approached by an out-of-state buyer as she left the store. She had just paid twenty dollars for two bottles, but was offered forty, and promptly accepted. This buyer, too, poured out the bourbon.

One wonders about investing in such items, however, when hearing the aftermath to many of these bottle stories. Ten days before the New Hampshire bottles were offered in the state liquor stores, they were advertised in national publications, empty, for fifteen dollars. Also, after the New Hampshire stores stopped selling them, supposedly the value on those sold would increase, as it was said no more would be made. Yet, a few months later, three hundred cases of the bottles were being sold in stores in Maine. While such activities must sell a lot of bourbon, they cast a shadow on serious collecting of the bottles at any great prices.

Other liquor companies have jumped on the bandwagon much less successfully, but as a result many interesting forms have been created that are bound to be of interest to future generations. This type of bottle making is not confined to liquor; we have had a detergent, perfumes, and other cosmetics packaged in bottles that have become collectible. It is difficult to advise anyone on whether to collect such bottles or on how much to invest in them, as no one knows what their future will be. I advise caution. The old bottles that were handmade will always rise in value—they have age and scarcity on their side.

Other concerns are turning out commemorative bottles with the likenesses of well-known people such as former President Kennedy and the late generals Eisenhower and MacArthur impressed on them. Some of these that sold new for five dollars are now on dealers' shelves at fifteen dollars. These bottles were never used to hold anything; they were turned out as decorative pieces. It is impossible to predict their future. In fifty years their value is bound to have increased. But if one wants to invest for the future, it would be wiser to invest in the quality old bottles, which will rise much more rapidly in value.

The subject of glass is the most provocative of any in antiquing. Whether a person buys old or new, he must be well advised. Reproductions of our early Burmese, Amberina, Mary Gregory, Peachblow, and so forth, by the glass factories in Murano, Italy, are not making collecting any easier. Most of these can be spotted immediately by long-time collectors, but many items will fool even experts. Our 1892 law made it mandatory for all imports to be marked with country of origin, and this was conscientiously practiced for years with suitable imprints that could not be altered or removed. But today most imported glass is coming into this country with paper labels only, and these are easily washed off. The National Association of Dealers in Antiques is working toward getting a label law that would make it mandatory to mold the name of the country of origin into all items.

Unlike furniture, glass was not limited by a particular design. All colors were used, and in combinations that excite present-day collectors as much as they did the original buyers. New England will introduce you to classic, artistic, and colorful forms of glass that can compete with that produced anywhere. There is no glass in the various categories made that has more value than New England glass. When you collect it, you are collecting the best available.

CHAPTER **4**

Earthenware and Porcelain

Wherever one digs among ruins, there will be examples of the potter's art in the form of old water and drinking vessels, shallow eating dishes, urns, and many types of food containers. Even during the days of the caveman, clay was fashioned into useful household artifacts and left to harden in the sun. When these pieces were exposed to fire while food was heating or water boiling, people discovered they hardened even more, and thus the art of the potter was born. The pieces hardened into an almost stonelike substance, and many years later became known as stoneware.

The technique of refining crude clay pottery into exquisite porcelains is credited to the Chinese. Marco Polo returned to Venice in 1295 after spending twenty-five years in China, and brought with him many examples of the refined pottery made there. From that time the potters and alchemists in Europe did all they could to imitate the quality and fragility of the Chinese work.

Decorated stoneware appeared in Germany in the early 1500's around Cologne and Coblenz. This brownish-red pottery took its color from the clay from which it was made. English work of this type did not begin until the early 1600's, and most of it was done in imitation of that being made on the Continent. British potters copied the method of combining ground flint with the clay, which when fired would produce a hard, brittle pottery. This at first was glazed with a lead glaze, which is opaque, and later with a salt glaze, which is clear. While a piece was being fired, salt would be thrown into the kiln. The salt, being converted instantly to a vapor under the intense heat, would coat the

80

piece being fired. This technique was used in this country until the past century, when more rapid and economical methods of glazing were discovered.

Some pieces were decorated with slip, or liquid, clay, and this procedure continued into the present century, making it difficult for the novice to determine age from technique of manufacture alone. Slipware of the late eighteenth and early nineteenth centuries is available, and is prized by collectors, but with later work done in the same crude manner, one must be careful to obtain positive identification. There is no easy rule or guide to ascertain age other than complete and satisfactory documentation of origin.

In this country, though we are very interested in collecting the stoneware of the past, we must content ourselves with that which appears for sale, and leave field treasures to the archaeologists, who are in a much better position to acquire them. At auctions and in shops appear many of the gray, red, and brown colored jugs, pots, crocks, milk pans, and similar products of both this and the last century. Regional items can be identified by the color of the clay. The types of decorations vary, but most potters used simple cobalt blue, which was colored on and then fired with the pieces.

Another form of decoration, "sgraffito," was less commonly used. This is the technique of covering a piece with liquid clay, or slip, of a color other than that of the pottery beneath. A design would be scratched through the slip to expose the original color. This technique was used first in China, then in Italy, where it received its name ("sgraffimento" means "incised outline"). Though many English, Dutch, and German potters decorated in this manner, very few in this country did so.

If you are buying stoneware, look for interesting shapes and fine decorations. Birds and flowers were used a great deal, with animals and geometric designs next in popularity. The value of pieces documented with makers' names and dates can be determined easily. Known pieces change hands from time to time, which helps to establish their prices; but unknown pieces must be treated individually, as far as setting a value upon them is concerned.

Because stoneware was made everywhere, it can be collected throughout the country. Much of it was shipped to areas where manufacture may have been limited, as is especially true of New England, where about 90 percent of the stoneware found came from outside the six-state area. Of the pieces manufactured in New England, most that is marked was made in Vermont. There is no question that some was made in New England, but because most of it is unmarked, documentation is difficult. Fortunately, these few pieces are durable, and many are in fine condition.

For an area so richly endowed with artisans of all types during our early years of colonization, it is surprising that much more significant work in earthenware and porcelain was not done. Apparently, most of it was imported well into the nineteenth century. And from then to the present day, only a few potteries have made their mark. Most of their early work is in museums or personal collections, and such pieces are there only because of factual documentation of their origin.

Earthenware may fall into several classifications. One is redware, which was barely more than a red clay baked and hardened. This might be glazed with a slip glaze hardened with heat so vessels could hold water without soaking it up. Stoneware was a refinement on the redware; it had flint mixed with clay, and was fired under intense heat to give it a stonelike quality. Then came molded, utility, and decorative wares that, by means of shape and design, aimed at beauty as well as utility.

Porcelain falls into three categories: china, Parian, and Belleek. Of the three, only Parian seems to have been made in quantity in New England. This is the white china made to simulate the Parian marble that was imported from the island of Paros for bust carvings and decorations. Josiah Spode in England created Parian china in the early part of the nineteenth century. It was made by several English potters and, later (1847–1858), by the Fenton works in Bennington, Vermont. China and Belleek were not products of the New England area, except for some unsuccessful attempts.

Some kitchen earthenware was made but none successfully until the latter part of the last century. A simple test to determine whether an object is earthenware or porcelain is to hold it to the light—if light passes through it, it is porcelain; if not, it is earthenware.

The Pilgrims utilized available clays to make pottery, and remnants of early redware have been dug up at Kingston. Indeed, old pottery remnants have been found just about everywhere early settlers, as well as Indians, went. Unfortunately, in New England, only remnants have been found, but they do show the imagination of the potters of those days, both settler and Indian. Colored glazes were used, and from these colors it is often possible to determine locale of manufacture. The Wadsworth Atheneum in Hartford has a good collection.

Dating pieces of stoneware seemed to take hold right after the Revolutionary War. Pieces dated as early as the 1790's were made by Abraham Mead of Greenwich, Connecticut. Some Boston stoneware is dated 1804, but with no maker's name or initials. In Hartford, Peter Cross began signing his work as early as 1807.

Surprisingly, with the exception of a few attempts in the Philadelphia area, this country did nothing to challenge the English domination of porcelain manufacture until the latter part of the nineteenth century, and even now imported china is still considered the most desirable in this country. The attempts by Bonin and Morris just before the Revolutionary War, and Tucker in the 1830's in Philadelphia, were the only serious threats to English supremacy up to that time. The American Pottery Company in Jersey City did work during this latter period but did not survive.

The Captain John Norton pottery was set up in Bennington, Vermont, in 1793, to make stoneware. It stayed in business until 1894. In the same community, Christopher Webber Fenton opened a pottery in 1847. As far as early manufacture of pottery was concerned, his was New England's outstanding work. Fenton made the lovely Parian ware, Rockinghamware, and all kinds of colored porcelains and graniteware. He is also credited with making the rare scroddleware.

In his book *How to Identify Benningware Pottery*, the director-curator of the Bennington Museum, Richard Carter Barret, reveals that only about one-fifth of the work of the Fenton Pottery was marked. He explains that too often collectors use the term Bennington in referring to all types of wares made there. Each pottery should be credited for the work it did.

Bennington turned out more beautiful work in porcelains and earthenware than any other place in New England. If you are a collector, its work is the best available in this area. A trip to the museum will give you an education on how important and how impressive such pottery wares were during the last century.

A modeler, Daniel Greatback, came to the Fenton Works in 1851 or 1852, and participated in the creation of some of its animal figures, as well as other designs. He is credited with doing the hound-handle pitchers that were first made in Jersey City where he had worked, and there is every indication that he did the famous Bennington pitcher of the same design and name. Mr. Barret reveals how to identify this pitcher: the Bennington hound's nose touches his paws, and there is space under his neck large enough to insert one's little finger; the hound must have a link collar; the underside of his body must have a sharp mold line; and his ribs should be felt even if not seen. Mr. Barret stresses that all four points must be identified; if any one is missing, it is not Bennington. In addition he has done much to dispel the notion that the plentiful Rebecca at the Well Rockinghamware pitchers were made in Bennington.

Though Bennington Parian was unmarked so it would be mistaken for English manufacture, since imports commanded better prices, there are ways to identify such pieces. Because grapes were popular for designs during the Victorian Period, they were used extensively on Parian on both sides of the Atlantic. But the English grapes are smaller and more delicate. The larger grapes are Bennington. Furthermore, there was much more iron pyrite in the soil in Vermont, and despite all efforts to

Bennington Parian pitchers in grape design; the one on the left is decorated with cobalt blue. *Bennington Museum, Bennington, Vermont.*

Bennington Rockingham-ware hound-handled pitchers. The open space under the neck denotes its origin. *Bennington Museum, Bennington, Vermont.*

◀

Bennington ware: (top, left to right) flint enamel change cover, "Swiss Lady," used to hide returning change at a bar; scroddled ware tulip vase; blue and white trinket box; scroddled ware slop jar; Parian porcelain trinket box; scroddle ware tulip vase; flint enamel spoonholder; (bottom row, left to right) blue and white cottage vase with applied grapes; Rockingham pedestaled vase; scroddled ware book flask; Sandwich glass clambroth font; flint enamel baluster pedestal, Rockingham step base; and another cottage vase. *Bennington Museum, Bennington, Vermont.*

Bennington Rockingham-ware dog. *Bennington Museum, Bennington, Vermont.*

Bennington stoneware with impressive cobalt-blue designs. The large one was made as a water cooler for the Hotel Putnam, Bennington. *Bennington Museum, Bennington, Vermont.*

screen out the matter, small specks of it would often turn up in the snow-white pieces. English wares are perfectly free from such imperfections.

The Bennington potteries turned out much graniteware similar to English ironstone china, and this is found in chamber sets, dinnerware, and utility pieces. Much of it was decorated, some with handpainting and gilding. Because most of it is not marked, one must study the forms and designs at the museum to judge any of this ware accurately.

Perhaps the next most important potteries were those operated first in Chelsea, Massachusetts, and then in Dedham under the guidance of Hugh Robertson. Between 1884 and 1895, he turned out what we generally refer to as "Dedham Pottery." His most famous achievement was the re-creation of the old Chinese oxblood glaze and crackleware. So important was his work that at the time of the closing of his plant, pieces were found on his shelves priced as high as $5,000. Today, an oxblood piece would sell at a premium, as only three hundred of them were made; but it is unlikely any will turn up. In addition he turned out redware pieces, along with art-carved designs that became very popular. The markings CKAW referred to the firm's original name, Chelsea Keramic Art Works. Robertson's name might appear in markings, as well as "Chelsea Faience."

In 1892 a contest was held in Boston to encourage the creation of new figures and designs. A rabbit design by a teacher, Joseph L. Smith, was chosen for its originality, and the rabbit was used extensively in the decoration of dinner plates. The "reverse" rabbit (headed counterclockwise) border is very rare. These were first made in raised molds with the figures raised, and painted accordingly. But these, being fragile, were discontinued in favor of a smooth mold with the designs painted on. These were done on the crackleware pieces, which collectors consider fine examples of potters' work at that time. Other motifs, of animals, flowers, and birds, were used extensively. Most have the rabbit trademark on the base, along with the name Dedham Pottery. Though these items keep turning up at flea markets and shows, their prices keep rising. Since these are desirable quality wares, and the pieces keep disappearing from the market, don't be concerned about paying a high price; the value will continue to rise.

I have a letter from a Mrs. Mary Fairbairn of Concord, New Hampshire, who writes: ". . . I worked with Mr. Hugh Robertson in Dedham

Pottery. He insisted I go to Boston to see the play *The Middle Man* to give me an idea of how he struggled to obtain the Ox Blood color for vases. I was young at the time and never dreamed the ware would become antique. He told me he won a prize at the Paris Exposition and was very disappointed not to have won first prize. He gave me a vase and I regret I haven't the slightest idea where it disappeared. It had elephant handles and a rose, separate petals on the front of the vase. I painted in a room with Mr. Robertson. Every rabbit was different. I recalled the lily plate and orange tree plate; also the crab and lobster. He had a Thanksgiving plate, too, turkey and cranberry; also a grape plate. Of course, the rabbit was the trade mark. He would get after me if I drew a rabbit too perfectly as there were no two exactly alike; all were hand drawn."

The Hampshire Pottery was founded in 1871 in Keene, New Hampshire, by James S. Taft. It was located there because of the excellent clays and silicas in the area, but later much material was imported from as far away as Europe. Their early products were the usual type for a rural pottery: stone jars, pots, pitchers, bowls, and the like. In 1883 a new kiln was erected to fire decorative pottery, and Mr. Wallace King was hired to create new designs and styles, such as tea sets, majolica, vases, and so on. The firm created many souvenir pieces with lithographed scenes that were quite popular with tourists. The colored ones were done by hand, and are real collectors' items. Because a Japanese artist was hired, there are Oriental motifs and raised designs on many Taft pieces. After World War I, the plant made ordinary white china for the restaurant trade and also brought out a line of ceramic tiles.

Some of the markings to look for are "J. S. Taft"; "James S. Taft"; "James S. Taft and Company, Keene, N.H."; "J.S.T. & Co."; "Hampshire Pottery"; and possibly "Hampshire," alone. Though there was a large output of wares from this plant, surprisingly, not much has turned up. It's possible that much of it was unmarked, making identification guesswork. One auctioneer in New Hampshire says that in eighteen years he has sold but one marked piece.

Another point of identification is the Royal Worcester finish given to decorated pieces. This would have been done over floral decorations painted on white china—giving them a look similar to their English counterpart. It is not difficult to tell the Keene majolica from the Etruscan from Phoenixville, Pennsylvania, since the Etruscan designs are well catalogued. The Keene pieces, done mostly in blue, yellow, brown, and green, with raised colored designs, can be recognized quickly.

Pieces found with the mark of an *M* inside an *O* were designed by Mr. Taft's sister, Mrs. Emmo Robertson, whose husband joined the firm in 1904. In 1916 Mr. Taft sold his plant to Mr. George Morton of Boston, who operated it until its closing in 1923. Mr. Taft died that same year. There was much experimentation in different compositions and designs, and quite possibly many one-of-a-kind pieces are unidentified by their owners. A particular form is that of a china that looked like opaque glass. It could be mistaken for Oriental work, of which it is a perfect imitation.

A very noteworthy pottery that is still making history in New England is the Dorchester Pottery. It is just south of Boston proper, off Morrissey Boulevard, on Victory Road. Founded by George Henderson, who came from Connecticut in 1895, after working in ceramics there, the plant has always made excellent stoneware. Most of it is unmarked by the maker, but can be identified by the names of the concerns who used his jugs, crocks, and pots as containers for their products. Because many of these concerns were Boston based, there is much Dorchester Pottery to be found in that area.

The clay from which it is made still comes from near South Amboy, New Jersey, and the cobalt used for the blue coloring is imported from Germany. A salt glaze was applied to waterproof the wares, but this technique ceased in 1914, when a new kiln was built. Once salt has been used for glazing in a kiln, no other glaze may be used. At present a Bristol glaze is employed that is clear and tough.

Mr. Henderson tried to buy the drying boards from the defunct Boston and Sandwich Glass Company on Cape Cod. These are of apple wood, and would not warp or split under intense heat. The fine-patterned Sandwich Glass was placed on these boards in a heated kiln to cool slowly, without cracking. Since the owners wished only to sell the entire plant, Mr. Henderson purchased it and removed the huge boards, which are still being used in Dorchester.

The firm is now operated by Mrs. Charles Henderson, the daughter-in-law of the founder; her brother, Charles A. Hill, who is both the decorator and glazer; and her sister, Mrs. Yeaton, who assists in the sales. Nando Ricci, the potter, and Mr. Hill, who have been making these decorated wares since 1940, sign all their work.

The firing of the kiln is a great event. Faithful customers mark their calendars with the date the kiln will be emptied, so they can be first at the door to walk off with their new prizes. Most of the designs are done in floral and geometric motifs, and one may still buy jugs, cups and saucers, tea sets, bean pots, and the like, decorated with scrolls, lace patterns, fish, and fruit. Pieces made as recently as ten years ago are commanding top prices well over their original worth. They may be found from time to time in shops and at auctions.

Among the old pieces the firm has on display is a switchel jug. This stands about fourteen inches high, and is about nine inches in diameter at the base. It has a very wide mouth and spout, and in it were put barley, rum, and molasses. The jug would be tied to the horse's harness as workers went into the field, so the mixture would be shaken up. Later, the field hands would nip at the concoction.

This is the last of the name potteries still engaged in the making by hand of decorated stoneware, and its output is highly recommended as a collectible that will quickly increase in value. It is sold only at the pottery. The supply is limited, and local demand is great. I hope that if this pottery ever goes out of business, some historical group will acquire

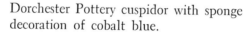

Dorchester Pottery cuspidor with sponge
decoration of cobalt blue.

Dorchester Pottery casserole in pine-cone
pattern.

Dorchester Pottery with cobalt-blue decoration, Thalia design. Signed by C. A.
Hill; the potter was N. Ricci.

Dorchester Pottery with cobalt-blue decoration, clematis design. Signed by C. A. Hill; the potter was N. Ricci.

Dorchester Pottery: covered pot in pinecone design; handled mug with clown.

Old Dorchester Pottery salt-glazed switchel jug, circa 1900.

Dorchester Pottery with cobalt-blue decoration: (left to right, top row) scroll, fantasy, blueberry; (left to right, bottom row) striped, pine cone, clematis.

the premises as a place to show some of the firm's work. In this pottery history is being made today, and deserves preservation.

There is a great rise in interest in Chinese ceramic art, both old and new. New England has maintained its interest since the first clipper ships sailed around the Cape to begin our trade with the Orient. Wealthy people in the seaport cities used much of this china for their tables and for decoration in the eighteenth century. But Chinese ceramics have been with us a long time, and there are several possible reasons for the growing interest in them. Perhaps the younger and affluent antique collectors are buyers whose tastes tend toward Oriental designs; or it may be that Chinese exported pieces are getting short in supply and thus higher in price and that some people who feel nothing is good unless it is expensive are becoming interested. Furthermore, because it is impossible to import Chinese antiques from Red China because of our political and trade barriers, the incentive to possess something that in effect has been smuggled in through trade with another country must have its effect.

For centuries, Chinese graves were venerated, and no one would dream of violating one. But in due course many were despoiled, revealing that centuries ago a man was buried with his worldly possessions. Naturally, such artifacts aroused interest. Early Chinese pottery and porcelain have assumed great importance, and the United States led in the development of the fine art of imitating them. It took centuries before the Chinese techniques could be duplicated. Early Chinese treasures are valuable, and collectors diligently pursue them. Tourists in Hong Kong, Japan, Singapore, and Bangkok are discovering great supplies of early Chinese work that is being funneled out through these "windows to the West." Gravedigging must be a rewarding, though hazardous, avocation in Red China these days, and many American dollars spent on art and antiquity eventually reach that country.

In any event, the pieces without the "Made in China" stamp are the ones of interest now. Many forms of Chinese export porcelains are highly collectible, and eighteenth-century export porcelain is especially rewarding. There is more of it in New England than elsewhere in the country.

People wonder whether Lowestoft china and Chinese export are the same. We do know that in the early part of the eighteenth century there was a china-making firm in Lowestoft, England, that made many fine wares in the Chinese style, as did almost all the early potteries at that time. In addition, some of these makers imported china from the Orient and acted as importers and exporters, as well as manufacturers. It is difficult, therefore, to know where some of it was made; and to add to the difficulty, for years the English makers used the then popular Oriental motifs in their designs. Though the name Lowestoft has been loosely applied to all such work, it should not be. Much of the early Bristol, Worcester, Bow, and Chelsea made in England cannot be distinguished from Oriental except by an expert. However, some work can be identified, even by the newcomer. Rose Medallion, now more commonly referred to as Chinese five-color export porcelain, is a highly decorated ware, with more or less orange and red as base colors, and generally with greens and blues used for pictures and scenes that tell stories of Oriental life. Other highly collectible work includes Celadon, which is a light-green tinted porcelain, often highly decorated with flowers, and so on; Fitzhugh, which is basically a whitish-gray pottery with blue geometric-looking designs; and Cantonware, which is extremely heavy, has a grayish tint, with scenes sketched in blue, and is characterized by an inner border of blue half-circles. It is difficult to determine the age of many of these imports because they were made in the same manner for many years. These are the best types of china available in New England now.

But since the greatest demand for Chinese items probably is in New England, this area may not be the best place to get a good price. There is a good supply of old pieces here, but not as good a supply of the more recent ones, which are coming in to the West Coast. Early American homes were well supplied and decorated with Chinese wares because of New England's great trade with the Orient; since such pieces are very much in keeping with our period homes, there is a great demand for them. Dealers in metropolitan areas are better supplied, since country settlers were less interested in owning fine china, and most could not have afforded it anyway. There is an abundance of the durable Cantonware, as well as a good supply of the five-color; but because Celadon and Fitzhugh were less popular, not quite so much will be found.

English china of the eighteenth century is quite scarce, but the supply of nineteenth-century ware is plentiful. Unfortunately, these cannot always be obtained in sets because of breakage over the years, and buying incomplete sets with the idea of finding companion pieces is hazardous, to say the least.

Among the more popular dishes to collect are the "Historical Blues," which were turned out in abundance during the 1820's and 1830's. Potters in England grouped together in Staffordshire County, an area with excellent clays and water, and from there came a series of dishes and sets that rank high as collectible items. Painters and other artists were commissioned to draw scenes of important buildings, harbors, waterworks, historical events, battles, and landscapes, as well as pictures of famous people. Faneuil Hall in Boston, Fairmount Park in Philadelphia, Lafayette's landing at Castle Garden in New York, Captain McDonough's victory over the British on Lake Champlain were but a few places and events immortalized on these plates. At one time these were plentiful in New England and other parts of the country, but today they are scarce.

Another series of "Historical Blues" was turned out in the 1890's, and came in numbered sets. Though pieces turn up frequently, complete sets are rare, and those who own them rarely part with them. This series is dated, so it is not difficult to tell the pieces from the early blues, even

Rare English washstand set in berry motif with gilding. The bottom piece is a pouring pitcher. *Chase House, Strawberry Banke, Portsmouth, New Hampshire.*

if you know little about old china. Pictures by traveling artists would be reproduced on decals, or "transfers," as they were called, and applied in blue color to the plates. Most of the glazing over this was good, but mass production did result in some poor surfaces filled with imperfections and smudged designs. Some interesting mistakes occurred, and high prices are being paid for plates with them. On the plate commemorating the landing of the Pilgrims, the first issue showed the ocean waves running at a ninety-degree angle to the shore. This was corrected in later issues, but the first ones have become extremely valuable.

While it is late to start collecting old china from the standpoint of getting any bargains, it does make sense to start collecting those of the nineties or even those that are being turned out today. Wedgwood in England is still making commemoratives to be sold by churches, at tourist areas, in museums, and at historic restorations. These plates are blue, and of fine quality. Already those sold a few years ago have risen in price when resold. They will have an important place on the shelves of future collectors, since many of the landmarks depicted on them may not be in existence some years from now. Most such plates sell in the $2.00 to $2.50 price range, and are well worth the investment. Many are sold in New England. If you come from another part of the country, you can make an easy profit on them just by taking some home to sell to collectors who may never travel here.

Early English wares are well marked, and books are available that list pottery identification marks. Thomas Whieldon was the first successful English potter of note, and he had the good fortune to have Josiah Wedgwood and Josiah Spode working for him at the same time. These men went on to form their own potteries, which are still in business today, turning out some of the world's best porcelains and earthenware. Wedgwood and Spode are the dominant names in the world of china now, as they have been for many years. They have provided much of the china for the world's royalty, as well as for the common man, which is a tribute to their imagination. Their chinas, old or new, are always a good investment. Some of their patterns, though made for over a hundred years, are still in open stock, making it easy to fill in.

Actually, the best place to buy new English china and pottery is in Canada, where there is no import duty. Much of this is still turned out by hand. Irish Belleek, as well as Scottish stoneware, is plentiful and colorful. If you cannot find the old china to collect at prices you can afford, do not hesitate to buy new china that is handmade. These are the collectibles of tomorrow.

Europe furnished some of the finest porcelains ever to come to these shores, but they did not arrive in great quantity. They were more expensive than comparable work, and as a result the market was fairly limited here. Among the more favored pieces are those that bear the Limoges stamp. This is a center of china making in France. In the 1840's, David Haviland, a china importer from New York, made a trip to Limoges, and was so impressed with the work being done there that he bought a factory and made fine china for export to this country. He revolutionized manufacturing techniques, and all the potters there copied from him. However, China bearing Haviland's mark is the best to collect.

Next in importance are the porcelains that were made in Germany. These are very difficult for the average newcomer to distinguish from French ware. The bisque pieces, too, are hard to identify if unmarked. But since the prices on these pieces are about the same, knowing the country of origin is not too important.

Fine Dutch delft, Brittany stoneware, and the Capo di Monte pieces from Spain and Italy also are good collectibles.

CHAPTER 5

Clocks

THE hunting ground for early American clocks is still the northeastern section of this country. They are still to be found in homes in Pennsylvania and New York, but mostly in New England. Connecticut was the site of mass clockmaking, and probably more than half of those collected today came from there. While Connecticut clocks do not command the highest prices today, nor were they the first clocks made, they are the most abundant.

An amazing number of clockmakers lived in Connecticut, and one wonders how they received their training. Most of them seem to have been self-taught, and not all served as apprentices to established firms. Almost anyone mechanically inclined could build one of the early primitive clocks with a few tools for metalworking. As a result, blacksmiths, silversmiths, carpenters, and even gunsmiths took up the trade.

Actually, during the eighteenth century, most of the clockworks were imported from England in cases, and assembled here. Almost all the faces were imported, as well as the hands and pulleys. Therefore the local clockmaker was often only an assembler of parts. With crude tools, he could fashion pendulums and make weights by soldering sheets of tin into can shapes, filling them with whatever heavy material was at hand. American clock weights probably contain more kinds of fillings than a pie factory. Into some would go lead shot, and into others, scrap pieces of brass, iron, or other metals; soapstone or gravel might be used; and in the case of makers near the coast, beach sand made an excellent filler.

Early makers used ordinary gut to string the weights that would power the clock. As a result, many an unhappy housewife has heard a crash in the night as a worn gut gave way, allowing the weight to demolish the bottom of the clock, spilling out rusty old iron or sand as the seams split. That is why in most weight-driven clocks the gut has been replaced with flexible brass cable. This does not diminish the value of an old clock.

During the eighteenth century the tall, or grandfather, clock and shelf and mantel clocks were imported from England. Most local makers seemed to concentrate on the tall clocks, but men such as Simon Willard in Roxbury, Massachusetts, were working on smaller designs. Tall clocks could be made with an eight-day movement, because the weights had a long way to drop to the floor, and could thereby power the clock for that length of time. The shelf clocks, which were smaller, provided a much shorter space in which the weights could drop, and generally most of them would run no more than thirty hours. Once mass production made the spring-wound clock practical, weight drives gradually disappeared.

Many people think a clock with wooden works is necessarily older

Rare Simon Willard pendulum clock. The clockworks and bell swing as a pendulum. *Shelburne Museum, Inc.*

than one with brass works. The making of wooden works was an experiment made first by Eli Terry in Connecticut. He was seeking a cheaper method of manufacture, and some say he experimented with wooden works as early as 1808. Chauncey Jerome and Seth Thomas are two others credited with experimenting with wooden works. All soon gave it up, as these timekeepers were unreliable and difficult to repair.

Advances in machine-cut brass gears soon made the use of wood unrealistic. It is said that Terry was so skilled, he could cut a wooden gear without using a pattern. Sometimes rarity commands an inflated price, but, as rare as they are, wooden clock movements are not a good long-term investment. Though they are interesting curios, and someday may rise in value, today they are selling for about one-third the price of their brass counterparts.

Benjamin and Samuel Bagnall were probably two of New England's first clockmakers. They worked in Boston early in the eighteenth century. From their work we can see how little the style and shape of tall clocks changed from their day until a hundred or more years later, when such clocks went out of fashion. Other clockmakers of the early years

Pillar-and-scroll clock, Eli Terry, East Windsor, Connecticut, circa 1820. *Shelburne Museum, Inc.*

were William and Thomas Claggett of Newport, Rhode Island; Thomas Johnson of Haverhill, Massachusetts, David Blaisdell of Amesbury, and Gawen Brown of Boston.

Eighteenth-century clocks are scarce on the open market, but those that came after 1800 keep turning up for sale. Therefore, for all practical purposes, today's collector should concern himself with the later period. Tall clocks were made until the middle of the nineteenth century. Their decline was due to changing tastes, the abundance of less expensive mass-produced clocks, and the inconvenience of moving the tall ones (they had to be completely dismantled). Today, though they are no less inconvenient to move, we are willing to put up with the inconvenience for their value as antiques.

Many people wonder at the differences in clock values, and cannot understand why two clocks which are of the same period and look quite alike may be separated in value by several thousand dollars. There are good reasons. Handwork in construction is most important; clocks whose creators cut out each piece by hand have added value. Then, too, a clock must measure up in quality, taste, design, and construction. Age, of course, counts too.

Tall clock by Benjamin Clark Gilman, 1763–1835, Exeter, New Hampshire. Gilman was a silversmith, engraver, builder, hydraulic engineer, clockmaker and watchmaker, merchant and landlord. Cup finials, arch door, and plain body without quarter columns date this clock before 1800. *Courtesy Charles S. Parsons.*

Some clocks by Simon Willard and his apprentices may still be available. They hand-constructed every piece that went into Willard's clocks, exclusive of the cases. Because he was a recognized American maker, his clocks are of greater value here than those done by any of his contemporaries abroad. Willard's were excellent timepieces in every way, and command the top dollar in American clocks today.

A fairly good clue for distinguishing an early unmarked imported clock from an American one is that, generally, the imported clocks are equipped with solid cast-iron weights, where the American ones generally had can weights. Furthermore, any clock with a pine, birch, cherry, or maple case must be American, since these are native woods. We used mahogany and walnut as well, but it is not too difficult to distinguish these from the European cases of the same woods. The finish on the European cases is generally heavier and darker. Yet these points of identification are not firm, for it is very possible to interchange works, weights, faces, and so on, to make up a hybrid clock, and over the years it is very possible that this has happened to many of them.

There are clocks in our native wood cases with can weights that may have an English manufacturer's stamp on their basic works. Such a clock is considered American, as it would be the product of one of our journeymen who bought his works abroad and assembled them here.

Some native clockmakers designed clockworks on their own, making parts that are seen in their clocks alone. This makes it possible to identify the maker, as long as his work has been catalogued. Though unmarked clocks do not have the value of documented ones, because of the scarcity of all old clocks, prices are rising. If you are considering buying an early tall clock, do not delay. Every year brings higher prices, and today they represent one of the better investments in antiques.

From about 1810 to 1860 the clock world was almost completely dominated by the Connecticut clockmakers. The partnership of Silas Hoadley, Eli Terry, and Seth Thomas was the beginning of their activities. They went on to change the habits of American life for a half century. Later, they separated, and each, along with his numerous contemporaries, contributed new ideas and production techniques that resulted in there being a clock of some kind in almost every American home. During this era of mass production, some of the finest collectible pieces were made. Fortunately, most clocks were marked, and identification should be easy.

The transition from the weight-driven clock to the spring-driven one was quite orderly, but a whole new breed of craftsmen had to be trained. Spring-driven clocks presented no difficulties to Europeans, who had been making them for centuries, but serious manufacture of them did not take place in the United States until the early part of the nineteenth century.

Not only did the clockmakers devise efficient means of mass production; they also developed new techniques in selling. At that time, a good tall clock might cost about one hundred dollars. When the new shelf clocks came on the market for about ten dollars each, and would run many days on one winding, it is easy to see why they were successful. Peddlers carried them in their wagons, and sold them from house to house all along the eastern seaboard, and many such clocks eventually went west with the covered wagons.

While members of the Willard family were concentrating on the fine banjos and highly decorated shelf clocks, the mass producers turned out the ogee-framed and coffin-cased types, with little thought to aesthetic design. There are so many designs from so many different makers that cataloguing them would be almost impossible. This type of manufacture continued into this century with clocks housed in gaudy wooden gingerbread cases. Cases were also turned out in iron, marble, china, and bronze. Many were made in Europe, but fitted with Connecticut clockworks, quite the reverse of a hundred years earlier.

During this time little or no inroads were made by European clocks, except for very expensive ones. Fine French mantel sets of clock and candelabra, as well as intricately built English tall clocks with all kinds of gadgetry, were unlike anything being made here, and were imported only by the wealthy. Clocks showing the phases of the moon, some topped by rocking ships, others equipped with loud chiming devices, appealed to the affluent.

It was not long before clocks were being offered as premiums for soap wrappers; thousands of small china boudoir clocks were distributed in this country, most of them with the cases made in Germany and works from Connecticut.

In the middle of the nineteenth century watchmaking became important in this country. Waltham and Elgin were first, followed by such people as Waterbury, Ingersoll, and Hamilton. The famous dollar pocket watches that turned up in the 1890's were first made by Ingersoll.

These remained the greatest sellers for several companies who turned them out until inflation after World War II made it impossible to continue them.

The year 1914 saw the advent of the electric-powered clock, and with it the end of an era. Many of the fine wall clocks made for public institutions began to disappear, because winding them was inconvenient. Edward Howard of Boston, by himself and with associates, made some of the finest institutional clocks. These were made in banjo and figure-eight styles, and each style came in five sizes, ranging from about thirty inches to five feet. Today, these are still superb timepieces despite their age, and a Howard movement has never been known to wear out. Some are still in use in the Greater Boston area in banks and offices of old established companies. Most of the Howards that were in railroad stations have long since gone, as passenger stations have disappeared one by one. Some collectors have assembled all sizes of the clocks in each design, and these are very impressive when seen hanging side by side. Some of the Howard movements are being used in reproductions of tall clocks and in the smaller grandmother clocks being turned out by craftsmen. The old name on the dial is impressive. Howard made clocks in all styles; some of his best were made as large hanging timepieces for jewelry stores. Often the pendulums were hung on bars of different metals that would expand or contract with changes in temperature so that the pendulum length could never change or cause incorrect time. Howard clocks, still available, are excellent timepieces to collect; while the earlier clocks are so scarce substantial means are required to afford one.

In addition, among the early unmarked clocks may be some that are practically identical to those of a well-known maker, and people quickly and incorrectly attribute them to such makers. Most fine clockmakers had many apprentices, who would often go out on their own and continue to make pieces in the manner in which they were taught. When buying a very expensive clock, it is best to purchase one that has the name of the maker on its face or is well documented by its former owners with a bill of sale, letter, or some other old writing that tells its history. It is hazardous to call an unmarked Sheraton-cased tall clock a "Willard type," since the description might apply to 90 percent of the clocks made. The similarity in design of most tall clocks of this period is very evident when one sees them side by side. One must be careful, too, in attribution by the quality of case alone. The cherry cases made by David Young of Hopkinton, New Hampshire, rival those of any case housing a Willard movement. And there were a great many other fine cabinetmakers.

Almost every kind of clock ever sold in this country after 1800 is available in New England today. Enough money will part almost anyone from a treasured piece, yet today's prices are nowhere near what they will be in the not too distant future. Quality pieces will rise more rapidly, but there are a lot of sleepers in clocks today that will experience good increases. Among them are the calendar clocks that were popular at the end of the last century. These are still available for less than $100. They are functional oddities. The figure-eight school clocks, with which Seth Thomas must have made a million dollars, are in demand, yet prices are reasonable. Right now, these are the poor man's banjo clock—the one that takes the place of the desired Aaron Willard or Lemuel Curtis. They run eight days on one winding, and are quite accurate. Mantel chime clocks, some with Westminster or Canterbury chimes, or even ship's bells, will always climb in value. Less interest is evinced in the plentiful iron or marble or black wooden painted mantel

One of two known acorn clocks, made by the Forestville Clock Company, Bristol, Connecticut, with a view of the Hartford State House, which has been preserved as a historic building. *Hammerslough Collection.*

Banjo clock made about 1840 by James Cross, Rochester, New Hampshire, as he followed Edward S. Moulton and James Cole in that city. It has an eight-day brass weight-driven movement. *Courtesy Charles S. Parsons.*

"Gingerbread"—under that title the E. Ingraham Co. made clocks in Bristol, Connecticut, from 1884. This model is "Gila": It has a stamped wooden case with a calendar attachment; on the left is a barometer, and on the right, a thermometer. *Courtesy Charles S. Parsons.*

Mantel clock made by the Ansonia Clock Co., in Connecticut from 1852 to 1878 and until 1930 in New York City. The patent dates are 1881 and 1882. It has a metal case and an eight-day spring-wound movement with outside escapement. *Courtesy Charles S. Parsons.*

A tall clock by James C. Cole of Rochester, New Hampshire, 1815. Pine and maple case.

clocks that are rectangular in shape. China-cased clocks, products of this century, have also risen in value, and will continue to do so.

Occasionally, a tower clockworks taken from a town hall or church that has been demolished will turn up for sale. What to do with one is a good question. They are fashionable neither in our new churches and town halls that are being built to resemble Lego block construction charts, nor in our Colonial designs. But the old tower clocks are bound to rise in value for use in restorations and to replace worn-out ones. One of them is money in the bank if you can buy it and hold on to it for a few years.

One word of advice about purchasing an old clock—before you go out to buy, be sure you know of a repairman close at hand who can fix it. Some are dependent on whatever parts they may accumulate from auctions and estates, on buying up old clockworks, and possibly on the contents of an old clockmaker's shop. Others have machinery with which they can turn out needed gears. If you have no such craftsman in your area, think twice about owning an old clock.

Before buying, check the clockworks itself. None of the early ones were made with jeweled movements, so obviously there has been wear where metal has rubbed against metal for years. Get to the works, and try to jiggle the wheels and gears to see if they are loose where they rest in the frame. If they are too loose, this will affect the time and striking, and may result in a costly rebushing of the entire works to bring it into condition. A job of this type will approach a hundred dollars, so consider this in your prospective purchase. Such repair will save the clock, and generally make a good one of it, but its value should be adjusted accordingly. In the interests of preserving these old clockworks, I have hoped that some enterprising company would bring out jeweled pinion points that could be inserted into the old frames to stop wear. Just as with replacing the old gut weight hangers with brass cable, I should not think putting jeweled points in would lower a clock's value.

The collection of old watches is an ambitious project. Perhaps the most valuable ones are those made in Europe, which predate our fine watches by many years. Although inventories of estates list the watches made here as early as 1800, none are to be found. With our watch industry getting such a late start, we must content ourselves with some of the key-wind pieces made prior to 1865 as the earliest type to collect. Dealers have watched the rise and fall of prices on these key winds, and right now they have leveled off at a price still less than that of the better gold watches that followed them. Most of the key winds came in silver cases, and they still keep turning up with frequency in New England. A good early Ingersoll dollar pocket watch in running condition might well be worth more than an earlier key wind because of its scarcity. Longevity was not built into these, and low supply has made them costlier.

Unfortunately, it seems that some dealers are buying gold case watches because of the value of the metal in them, and then are scrapping them to be melted down. This will enhance the value of those that remain, so keep any gold-cased watches marked 22K or 24K.

Railroad watches, which were noted for their accuracy, are an entire field of collecting in themselves. Practically every concern turned out such a watch to enlist the public's confidence in its ability to produce an accurate watch. (Today, of course, we use radio or TV to check the accuracy of a timepiece.)

I know of a situation where at a military base a cannon was fired at retreat at five each afternoon, and the citizenry of a nearby town would check their timepieces. A town jeweler had a fine jeweler's clock in his window that was used by passersby as a reference for accurate time. One day a traveling salesman called the jeweler's attention to the fact that his window clock was fifteen minutes slow. The jeweler said that that was impossible, as he used the five o'clock cannon to check it every day. The salesman traveled out to the nearby base to investigate. The sergeant in charge said there could be no error, as he always checked his watch every day with the jeweler's window clock. The sergeant's watch must have stopped fifteen minutes on the way back to the post one day—no one knows when—and the whole community, as a result, had been running behind the rest of the world because of the confidence they had both in the jeweler and in the cannon.

CHAPTER **6**

Silver, Iron, Copper, Tin, Pewter, and Brass

EVERY civilization has used malleable metals to make utilitarian as well as ornamental devices. The early New England settlers hastened to set up forges to work the raw materials at hand for the basic necessities of life, then later turned their talents to luxury items. Very little documented seventeenth-century work has survived, and that which has is high in price.

In 1646 an enterprising group set up the Saugus Iron Works, as we know it today, to process the bog iron that still can be found on the Saugus marshes. The works has been magnificently restored to its original condition by iron and steel companies for about one and one half million dollars. Many years were spent in research, checking records and writings that referred to the site, and archaeological teams were employed to search for traces of foundations, tools, and machines that had lain buried since the works closed in 1670. They were concerned with the most minute detail, and even searched for a suitable oak tree large enough to be milled into a shaft for a water wheel—after a long search they found one in a forest in Maryland. The original huge five-hundred-pound hammerhead was found, showing that the works was well equipped to turn out large pieces in wrought iron. Slitting and rolling mills were part of the installation, which enabled the colonists to turn out sheet metal.

Iron, found in Braintree, Nahant, and Reading, Massachusetts, was shipped to the mill, which at that time was called Hammersmith. Charcoal was made in kilns in nearby forests. A similar operation was

111

under way in Braintree at this time, but records show that it never progressed far enough to be a going concern. Iron sheets and bars from the works were shipped throughout the colonies, where local iron-mongers and blacksmiths turned the raw material into useful tools and household artifacts.

Bog iron has been found in many sections of New England, and blacksmiths would refine this almost pure metal themselves, and work it into household utensils such as tools, lamps, candleholders, snuffers, tongs, and so on. One such well-known deposit is at Crystal Lake in Gilmanton Iron Works, New Hampshire. In adjoining small ponds, men would go out in flat-bottom boats to pick up chunks of bog iron from the bottom with long iron tongs. Three fairly large blacksmith shops in the area used the iron, and one of them developed the first iron plow with iron blades. This shop was later moved and expanded to become the huge Hussey Manufacturing Company in North Berwick, Maine, which is world famous for its bleachers, which are in major stadiums everywhere. In this area, iron was also mined from Gunstock Mountain in great quantities, but the high cost of extraction, as well as competition from the West, put the enterprise out of business. With the new equipment available today, mining might again be profitable, but the terrain has changed considerably; the well-known Gunstock Ski Area sits atop the slopes, and the white gold in the form of snow is worth much more than the black iron that lies beneath.

Connecticut claims to have played a part in the creation of one of the most important iron pieces in our colonial history. During the Revolution, a great chain was made and stretched across the Hudson River at West Point, during the navigable times of the year, to stop British ships from sailing north to the Albany area. Fourteen links of this famous chain have survived and are on display at West Point, along with a swivel and clevis. The chain was formed at the Sterling Iron Works just southwest of Sloatsburg, New York, and all of the chain's links came from there. The stories that different links for the Great Chain were made at different ironworks and assembled at the Hudson are untrue. They probably refer to a little-known, lesser chain that was stretched across the river at the Twin Forts of Popolopen Creek, five miles south of West Point, during 1776–1777. The forts fell to the British on October 6, 1777. Iron for this chain came from many places, one of which is believed to be the Salisbury Furnace at Salisbury, Connecticut, an area rich in iron.

Of all the metals, iron is the most difficult to document for age, because so much of it is still being worked today. Because of this, and because names of famous makers are not attached to pieces, iron artifacts will never command great prices. There are many blacksmiths today who will turn out andirons, fire tools, hinges, railings, pots, and the like, in the handcrafted manner of their forefathers. If these are put out to rust and age a few years, even an expert would be hard put to identify the old from the new. Because of this, iron items often languish in shops at low prices. For the same reason, metals other than gold, silver, and pewter (which generally were well marked) are held down in price, too.

This is about the only area of antiques where a hundred dollars would be a large price to pay for a good work of art. Very few pieces of iron, tin, brass, and copper sell for over a hundred dollars. About the only iron items that are worth more are the mechanical banks and some of the still iron banks that have risen in value recently. In copper and brass, weathervanes, chandeliers, andirons, and ornate fireplace screens and fenders can exceed this figure handily, but not all of them do. Brass whale-oil lamps are very rare, and pairs of good design that above all are in good condition will rise into the three figures. But this is a rather limited list of items in view of the quantity that must have been made in these metals over the span of years since the Pilgrims landed.

New England is full of iron objects of every kind. There are the large pig kettles that were used to scald the porkers before scraping off their bristles. The ones with legs and handles are more valuable than those without. Most of those found here today are brought in from Pennsylvania and the Midwest; they sell for about half the price in those areas. Perhaps dealers are simply bringing back many that originally had been sold here. Those with banding around the top and around the middle will rarely split. Check the legs on a solid surface, not outdoors or on sand or grass, as quite often they are so broken or worn the kettle will not balance properly. If they are rusty, remover or plain stove blacking will clean them. Many people paint them a flat black to stop further rusting; this does not lower their value.

Smaller iron kettles with handles are best when they have feet. Those with a six-inch protruding circle at the bottom were made to fit directly into the old kitchen wood ranges when the lid was removed. These are often called doughnut kettles, but must have been used for all types of cooking. By exposing the bottom directly to the flames below, it could be heated much more quickly.

Cooking utensils of all kinds, many in shapes we do not see today, are always turning up. Early waffle or biscuit bakers with long handles can be used in a fireplace today. Muffin tins in all shapes make excellent muffins, and many cooks still prefer iron to Teflon-lined aluminum or steel. Toast made in an iron rack toaster that stood before an open fire is much better than that cooked electrically. Many cooks still use the steak or chop broilers—hooks on an iron rack that allow the meat to be broiled in front of the fire without fat dripping down to fan the flames. Many restored country kitchens have walls on which these utensils are decoratively hung.

Iron candle and rush holders of Pilgrim times are quite scarce, and one must be careful of reproductions. Recently, many of these, as well as the Betty lamps, or crusies, were imported from Portugal, and are turning up well rusted in shops. The work is so good that the owners probably do not know they are new. As long as people are willing to accept them as old, perhaps no harm is done, so long as the pricing isn't unrealistic.

If you are concerned with age and authenticity, check iron bells carefully. The most likely points of wear are the pins on which the bell rides and the point at which the striker hits inside. Yet, it is possible to age a new one by salting it and leaving it outdoors to rust, making it look like an old bell that was never used.

Other iron items of interest are coffee roasters, popcorn poppers, and firepans, all of which are similar in some ways. The firepan is an iron-covered pan with a handle that was most often wooden. It was used to carry coals from one fireplace to another to start a new fire without repeating the long process of striking flint to tinder. Coffee roasters look practically identical, and perhaps the same utensil was used for both purposes. Popcorn-popper handles should show a great deal of charring next to the pan, where they would have been over the coals. If they do not, it is possible the handles have been replaced. Iron fireplace trivets were made in all shapes and sizes to hold kettles, and the large frying pan on legs, or spider, was used directly over the hot coals, with the feet giving it the elevation needed. Many of these items have been reproduced in recent years by manufacturers of "Americana," so if you are concerned about authenticity, check carefully.

Tinware was made much later than iron in this country. While we were still colonies, England controlled the supply of tin available, much of it coming from the British Isles itself, notably from Cornwall. Some was imported for the sanitary coating for rolled iron sheets. The rolling and dipping process was complicated. Blocks of iron were rolled into thin sheets and then dipped in tin to give them a clean rustfree coating that would not contaminate water or food. (The process later gave way to rolled steel coated with tin, resulting in the "tin" can as we know it today.) Prior to the Revolution, all tinware was imported from England—we had no facilities for making it here. Just before the Revolutionary War, facilities were installed in Connecticut and Massachusetts to make items needed for the Continental Army.

Early tin pieces were functional—such household and cooking equipment as reflector ovens; pierced footwarmers and lanterns; spice grinders and storage cans; tea and coffee cans; lamps, candleholders, and sconces; candle molds, and, of course, trays. The list is endless. The great era of tinware in this country spanned the entire nineteenth century, with heaviest production after the Civil War, when stoves replaced fireplaces and quick-heating pots and pans were in demand.

A notable area for collecting early decorated tinware is around Westbrook and Portland, Maine. Zachariah Stevens began the manufacture of tinware, decorated and otherwise, in Westbrook, which is just north of Portland. He and his sons, as well as other firms in the area, turned out a considerable amount of it. The noted pewterers Rufus Dunham and Allen and Freeman Porter worked for Stevens, then left to ply their trade in pewter, making this a great area to search for early pewter as well.

Because of our problems with excess refuse, we are turning more and more to disposable products. Soon the tin can and other containers will become things of the past as they are either replaced by plastics or materials that are self-disposable, as suggested by scientists. Cooking utensils, too, may soon disappear as electronic ranges come into widespread use to heat food instantly, in plastic bags, as some restaurants do now. Built-in coffeemakers will replace coffeepots and teapots, and canisters will no longer be needed. Such a generation would leave a limited heritage of artifacts such as paper and plastic bags, cups, dishes, and utensils.

Copper and brass are closely related, for brass really is a mixture of copper and zinc. They are soft metals that may be worked easily in sheet form with tin snips and hammer. Seams are easily soldered to make quick joints, and designs can be impressed by hammering the sheet against a molded form. Neither will rust, but if they are to come in contact with food, they must be tinned to avoid contamination. English domination in the area of copper and brass made it impossible for our native craftsmen to do more than limited work with these metals. Products made up to the present day are relatively inexpensive because few famous makers signed their pieces. Much handwork is still being done in these metals, and after a little patina (this comes with age) sets in, it is difficult for newcomers to tell the old from the new.

Copper and brass were used extensively in decorative pieces and in such functional pieces as bedwarmers, lamps and lanterns, fireplace equipment, buttons, and some cooking equipment. Those that probably command the greatest prices today are the weathervanes and signed fireplace pieces. The Hunneman name appears on good andirons that were made in Roxbury by this famous manufacturer of fire-fighting wagons and pumpers early in the nineteenth century. The Hunneman foundries cast many household items for family and employees, and some of these turn up from time to time.

Many brass candlesticks, mostly of English manufacture, turn up too. Some early (seventeenth- and eighteenth-century) Flemish brass candleholders may be found in New England at amazingly low prices. The low price is due to the millions of brass candlesticks made in the last century in exactly the same designs as the earlier ones. Since makers were unknown—as they still are unknown today—and the candlesticks were reproduced in such abundance, the prices are down compared to other antiques.

Many interesting copper and brass pieces in Victorian shapes have turned up. These have a marked resemblance to silver- and nickel-plated pieces, which is understandable, because many are the bodies of pieces that were originally silver- or nickel-plated. Plated pieces, blackened with age, are often inexpensive. You can either have them replated to bring them back to their original condition or have the old plating stripped to reveal the copper and brass beneath. All silver- and nickel-plated pieces are made of copper, brass, white metal, or all of these. Quite often they are handsomer with the plating stripped, and this process usually is less expensive than replating. The body of a teapot, for instance, most likely will be made of copper, which is easily molded and shaped. The handle, spout, feet, the finial on the cover, and possibly the cover itself will be made of brass. The metals will be soldered where necessary, and sometimes little care was exercised in how it was done, as the workmen knew the plating would hide their careless work. Yet, this crudeness sometimes has great charm.

Much Oriental brass and copper, dating after 1892, will be found in New England, most of it marked with country of origin. This is all handwork—much of it shoddy, much of it good. Values of these pieces are academic; they must be judged on the basis of how much you want them. The earlier Oriental pieces of good quality can command fairly high prices. Samovars are popular, as well as bells, Turkish coffee grinders, and hammered plaques.

Although brass and copper were used so extensively in New England, we are unable to credit particular craftsmen, with the exception of Hunneman. Some dealers have attempted to tout the names of brass and copper workers to increase the values of certain pieces, but the well-versed antiquarian has not been taken in. Though there are many contemporary craftsmen who have done good work in brass and copper, for the all-handmade period before 1830, documentation is available almost solely for imported items. After electrolytic plating came into being in the 1840's, much of the copper and brass ended up as plated items. There was little manufacture of products of brass and copper alone. Though craftsmen and firms turned out brasses for chests, candleholders, chandeliers, doorknobs, locks, and a multitude of other household items, none has risen to the forefront as an outstanding maker, nor did anyone create new designs. The nineteenth century brought forth little more than reproductions of old designs or of fashionable European imports. This is not a good area for investment. Few such items can possibly rise in value nearly as rapidly as items in other areas of antique collecting. Collect and buy copper and brass for its functional use and beauty. New England is a great storehouse for good pieces because of proximity to Europe and the importance of Boston as a seaport for many years.

There has been a marked increase in interest in bronzes. Most of those collected are European or Asiatic, and depict human or animal figures, flowers, and the like. These were originally sculpted and then cast in bronze (a mixture of copper and tin). The elegance of the work and the names of the creators set the prices. Some will be found with the Tiffany name on them, along with a mark that they were made in a country such as Russia. Not too many years ago, these were not high in price, but bronzes are "in" right now, and seem here to stay. Contemporary New England workers in bronze are commanding good prices for their work, but there is nothing made in this region in antiques to be concerned about. The French and Russian bronzes seem to be commanding the best prices. Do not get excited about the shoddy bronze-coated white metal figures that turned up in abundance during this century—many made in Japan and Germany. These have relatively little value. Many were made as lamp and clock bases with reclining figures of animals. Although they may look good at a distance, their poor quality shows when they are examined closely.

Early Oriental bronzes are excellent, but you won't find a great many. These have been divided into three eras: the first, pieces of the Shang-Yin Period, extended from ancient times to the tenth century B.C.; the second was the Chou culture, which extended from that time to approximately the seventeenth century (different scholars have set different dates), when trade with the West was still in its infancy; the third phase is known as the Ch'in or Huai Period, and extended from then until this century. Reproduction of earlier styles and greening of the bronzes by chemical means keep collectors wary when determining age. Much of the early bronze and copper was destroyed at times when all luxury metals were confiscated to be melted down to meet the demands of wars. At the time of her Revolution, France lost many metal treasures.

Gilded bronze, or "ormolu," dates from the end of the seventeenth century. It was and is used for decoration of furniture and as bases for porcelain pieces. Much furniture that is found in New England bears this type of decoration, and much of it is attributed to the French. But the United States and other countries produced ormolu too.

The fifteenth century brought with it the decoration of bronze by means of enameling. This technique was called "cloisonné." Liquid china stone was painted on to form decorative designs or scenes, and then fired. The eighteenth century saw a great demand for this work, and French missionaries brought the technique home with them from China. The work is a desired collectible. Most cloisonné found in New England is marked with country of origin, dating it after 1892. This is not so valuable as earlier work. All cloisonné is not necessarily good, so examine the piece before you buy. This is fragile work, and even thirty or forty years of use will give it a look of real antiquity.

A final note on brass and bronze: Brass beds are not solid brass at all, but rather brass-plated steel. The finials atop the bedposts, and possibly some fancy molded decorations, may be of the solid metal, but the rest of the frame is only plated. Prove this for yourself with a magnet —it will not stick to brass, but will to the steel.

Eighteenth-century American pewter is scarce because England controlled our supply of tin, which is nine-tenths of the content of pewter. The other tenth is generally copper, with, in later years, anti-

Prentis House kitchen, with important pine sideboard hutch, pewter measuring set, pewter plates, fine tavern table, and blanket chest with covered burl bowl on top. *Shelburne Museum, Inc.*

mony, bismuth, and sometimes lead added. Even after the Revolutionary War, little or no tin was shipped here, so the native pewterers had to depend on what they could salvage by remelting older worn pieces. The owners of the old pieces would let the pewterer keep one-third the weight of the scrap pewter. Thus most of our early American pieces were melted down to cast new ones. Much of the early English pewter was melted in the same way. The metal is soft; it will stand no direct exposure to heat, and wears away easily with usage. During the eighteenth century a harder form of metal, called Britannia, was created by the English, and this is the material in which the bulk of our collectible pewter is found today. Some people regard authentic pewter as those items that were cast in a mold, and Britannia as metal worked on a lathe over wooden forms cut to the desired shape. I do not feel this is wholly accurate, and it should not be regarded as a rule. In any event, one must regard all Britannia as pewter but not all pewter as Britannia.

There is a simple rule to follow in collecting—if the word "pewter" is spelled in any manner on the bottom or side of the piece, it is most likely very late and not really of any collectible value. We find many pieces with the words Colonial Pewter, Old American Pewter, Paul Revere Pewter, Best English Pewter, and so on. This seems to make some owners feel they have a rarity, especially if it is a piece with Revere's name on it. Though pewterers were diligent in stamping their touchmarks or names on the pieces, there are many fine unmarked pieces that can be attributed to American manufacture from the shapes and designs alone. This area requires a great deal of research and study, and I would not recommend it to the casual collector, who would do best to accept the judgment of a reputable dealer.

Interestingly, early American pewterers, feeling that the colonists believed foreign-made pieces were of better quality and workmanship, quite often would stamp LONDON on the bottom of their pieces. But they would make one of the o's look like a ǫ to lessen the wrath of their English cousins. Because the English responded by marking many of their pieces with the ǫ, whenever such pieces turn up today, one must look for other evidence when judging country of origin. John Skinner, a pewterer of Boston, who marked his pieces "Semper Eadam," his trademark, stamped many of his pieces LONDON, without the ǫ.

Every colony must have had its pewterer, for pewter utensils gradually replaced the woodenware or treenware that had been in general use. The seacoast cities benefited from trade with England and the Orient; they were able to import china and pottery to use in their homes. In the countryside, wood was still very common, but items such as mugs, spoons, and plates were more easily made by casting than by carving. Some consider pewter the poor man's silver. This is not wholly accurate—pewter was used, not to supplant silver, but to supplant wood and crude pottery. But it is true—and perhaps the basis for the statement —that church plates for the poorer country churches were pewter rather than silver as in the richer city churches. In any event, pewterers of those days left an interesting heritage of shapes and forms in functional pieces that increase in beauty and value as the years go by.

Perhaps the most common piece to be found is the porringer, followed closely by plates and dishes. The handled porringer was an eating bowl, and each member of the family would have his own. A plate can be up to nine inches in diameter; anything nine inches or over is a dish. The larger dishes are commonly referred to as "trenchers" or "chargers." The term "trencher" was used in early woodenware to describe a hollowed-out log that was used as a bowl for food. In old England, the man who carved meat at an inn was often referred to as a "trencher." *Webster's Third New International Dictionary* describes "charger" as an archaic word to describe a platter or serving dish.

Pewter is judged by the quality of its shape and form, the condition of its metal, and above all by any clear touchmarks of noted makers. Since eighteenth-century American pewter is scarce, it is advisable to collect imported pieces if you want early work. Most came from England, but there are examples from all over Europe, as settlers brought their possessions with them from almost every country. Church communion services, found in storage cupboards, having been replaced many years back with silver, turn up for sale from time to time. Cuspidors are very rare, but not in demand. Since pewter melts easily, and cannot be placed on a heated surface, its use was relegated to those artifacts that were used mostly in serving. Candlesticks, oil lamps, candelabra, and other functional pieces are rather scarce. More common are the plates, dishes, mugs, beakers, porringers, and teapots. Sugars and creamers aren't easily found.

As a general rule, old pewter is not used today except for decoration. It is impractical for everyday use because it wears so easily. While we might use practically every other type of early artifact, even the much more valuable silver, our old pewter is only to be admired. As for its care, some insist it should be washed with a detergent, leaving the old darkened look. Others claim that since it was originally a gleaming piece of metal, it should be restored to that state. If you do clean it, be sure not to buff it—it is best to leave the old marks and ridges to keep an aged look.

Early pewterers were plentiful in Connecticut, Rhode Island, and Massachusetts. Maine supplied a few known artisans, and New Hampshire and Vermont contributed but one family. Records of post–Revolutionary War pewterers, whose work extended well into the Britannia Period until the 1860's, reveal a Richard Lee, who worked in Grafton, New Hampshire, and later moved to Massachusetts and then to Springfield, Vermont. His son, Richard, Jr., worked there until 1815, and later moved to Beverly, Massachusetts, and then to Rhode Island.

Connecticut had perhaps the greatest number of early makers whose works are valued today. The most noted are members of the Danforth family, among them Thomas, Edmond, John, Joseph, Josiah, Samuel, and William, along with a host of sons and other relations who worked over a span of five generations from the 1770's through the 1850's.

Pewter, wood-handled ladle, by Richard Lee of Vermont, New Hampshire, and Massachusetts, who worked from 1770 to 1823. *Shelburne Museum, Inc.*

▶

Pewter Communion set by William Calder, Providence, Rhode Island, 1817–1856: Flagon, pair of chalices, and plate. *Currier Gallery, Manchester, New Hampshire.*

They worked generally in the Middleton and Norwich areas. Other noted men were Thomas Boardman and Samuel Hamlin from Hartford and later Providence; Ashbil Griswold from Meriden; and Thomas Derby and Jacob Whitmore from Middleton.

Rhode Island gave us William Billings, William Calder, and Gershom Jones, all from Providence; Joseph Belcher and his son David, and Samuel, Thomas, and William Mellville, from Newport.

There were many fine pewterers in Massachusetts, among them Richard Austin, George Richardson, Samuel Green, and Thomas Badger from Boston; Nathaniel Austin, Charlestown; Roswell Gleason, Dorchester; James Putnam, Malden; Israel and Oliver Trask, Beverly; and the two men who gave their names to a great concern still in existence today, Henry Reed and Charles Barton, from Taunton.

Westbrook, Maine, had an unusual colony of metalworkers headed by Rufus Dunham and his sons, and Allen and Freeman Porter. This seems to be the only Maine locality to have produced pewter in any quantity.

The above list can serve as a reference to names of makers whose works are most sought now. Unrecorded touchmarks turn up occasion-

Pewter mug and tankard, Nathaniel Austin, Charlestown, Massachusetts, 1763–1807. *Currier Gallery, Manchester, New Hampshire.*

Punch pot in quadruple-plate silver by Simpson, Hall and Miller Company, circa 1890.

ally, sending historians scurrying to archives and town records in search of documentation, and in this way finding new evidence. Clubs have been set up by collectors for the purpose of sharing valuable information.

Though silver is one of our basic metals, and has been in use about as long as civilized man has been in existence, there is very little of fine quality left to collect in New England. The very rare American pieces of the seventeenth and eighteenth centuries are mostly locked up in collections or held by families that will not sell them except under the most dire circumstances. Early English or other foreign silver has risen in value, but the work of native craftsmen commands greater prices than in any other field of antiquity. For instance, a Paul Revere three-piece tea set sold early in 1968 in New York at auction for seventy thousand dollars. Only the finest furniture has approximated a relative rise in value.

Our silverwork is directly related to that of England, again because our colonies were dependent on the mother country for supplies. British guilds made sure the finished silver product, and not the raw material, was shipped. But American craftsmen melted down the large English,

A silver tankard by Thomas Savage of Boston and Bermuda, 1664–1749. It was probably made before 1700 for the Paynter family. It has the Paynter arms on front. Height, 8½ inches; weight, 40 ounces. Very few pieces of Savage silver have ever been found. *Hammerslough Collection, Wadsworth Atheneum, Hartford, Connecticut.*

Dutch, and Spanish coins, and many ships laden with this metal were docked in New England ports. Furthermore, many Spanish merchant vessels on their way home, carrying cargoes from Mexico and South America, were overtaken by privateers. Were it not for such acts of piracy, we might have no American-made silver of the eighteenth century.

The silverworker of that time did not have a shop window and shelves full of merchandise waiting for customers to come in and buy. Silver was so costly that it was made only on the order of wealthy patrons who would not only pay for the work but supply the raw material as well. A boy would be apprenticed to a silversmith at the age of fourteen, and when he reached manhood, at twenty-one, he was free to open his own place of business, having been well instructed in his trade. Though we tend to think of craftsmen as looking rather elderly, like a Benjamin Franklin peering over the top of his spectacles, it is difficult to realize that some of the finest work collected was done by young men in their twenties. Paul Revere was thirty-three, in 1768, when he made what is considered the finest piece of early American silver in existence today, the famous Sons of Liberty bowl that is on display at the Boston Museum of Fine Arts.

Silver salver by Thomas Edwards of Boston, 1701–1775. Made for Richard Gibbs, it has Gibbs' arms on front and "R. Gibbs" on back. Diameter, 15 inches; weight, 53 ounces. This is an unusually large salver. *Hammerslough Collection, Wadsworth Atheneum, Hartford, Connecticut.*

One reason old silver has risen so greatly in price is that practically all of it is self-documented. The early English guilds of goldsmiths and silversmiths led the way to marking systems that enable us to pinpoint, at least back until 1479, the age of a piece within a span of twenty years. The 1335 requirement that a touchmark be stamped on pieces to show the maker was followed by a regulation in 1477 that a leopard's head be imprinted as well. Actually, it looks more like a lion, and is generally referred to as the "lion passant." He should always face to the left. In 1479 the system of using letters of the alphabet, changing their shape and form as needed to represent a span of twenty years, was instituted. The letter *J* was not used because it resembled an *I* too closely. In 1784 it became necessary to imprint a profile of the head of the reigning sovereign, and this held in effect until 1890, just before it became necessary to stamp the country of origin on silver pieces. The guilds guarded their ethics well, and on several occasions silvermakers were put to death for attempting to misrepresent the silver content of the items they had made. In the early days the necessary weight of silver in relationship to its alloy metals in coins was much lower than that for what we call "sterling." This was to frustrate those who would melt coins down for a supply of raw material, as the cost of making coins was very high and there always was a shortage.

Perhaps the reason touchmarks were used before initials or names were imprinted is that so many people were illiterate. Makers would use such symbols as stars, a moon, horse's head, eagle, or crown. They continued to use them even after the 1740's. The American silversmiths carried on the tradition of stamping initials, touchmark, or a name, but seemingly with less diligence than the English. This leads to a word of caution: evidence of alteration has been uncovered. English markings have been burnished out, leaving only initials, which might lead collectors into thinking they were purchasing American silver. In addition, the markings on the back of a spoon, for example, might be cut out and reset in the bottom of a more expensive teapot, with the work done so cleverly it is almost impossible to detect. Quite often by breathing on touchmarks you will be able to see the difference in silver quality and patina where it has been disturbed by such workmanship. No one knows how many pieces of early English silver that look almost exactly like ours in age and quality have American touchmarks embedded in their bottoms.

Since coffee and tea were not in general use in England until the middle of the seventeenth century, it was not until after this time that sets of silver pots, jugs, creamers, and sugars were made. The handles of the coffeepots were at right angles to the spout, while teapots had their spouts pointing directly away from the handles. (The difference between the chocolate pot and coffeepot is that the former had no spout.) Sugars and creamers did not appear until about 1700, and at that time they were not made as sets. The first tea or coffee sets all done in the same pattern were not made until about the time of our Revolution. People in the past have collected odd pieces of pre-Revolutionary silver and have made up sets that are in perfect keeping with the times.

Tea caddies appeared in different forms: some were individual pieces, while others were done in silver encased in mahogany or ebony boxes, so that several types of tea could be kept in separate compartments. These will often be found with locks.

One must check carefully for the remaking of a piece, even for remaking done years back. It may have been remade a hundred years ago to satisfy the needs of a particular person. In the early days of our country, women as well as men drank a considerable amount. Many women had their own mugs and tankards. During the early part of the last century, the temperance movement led to doing away with such drinking vessels; but, rather than discard old family relics, quite often they were remade by adding spouts and, if necessary, covers so the pieces could be used as tea or coffee pots. Later on, as the temperance movement abated, many mugs were restored to their original condition, and by such good craftsmen that it is almost impossible to detect the alteration. If you are interested in early quality silver, you should seek the advice of a skilled appraiser.

As a general rule, any piece of tableware, be it silver, china, glass, or pewter, is worth considerably more if it is footed than if it sits directly on the table. And feet are easily added to a piece of silver. There are no easy rules for determining if feet have been added—again, consult an expert.

The hand decoration of silver is done in several ways: by engraving the piece by cutting into it with sharp tools; by chasing, which is hammering in a design on the outside of the piece (sometimes directly against a carved mold) with small punches and chisels; and by repoussé, where the hammering of the design is done from the inside of the piece. The gadroon border—a continuous design of curved half circles, referred

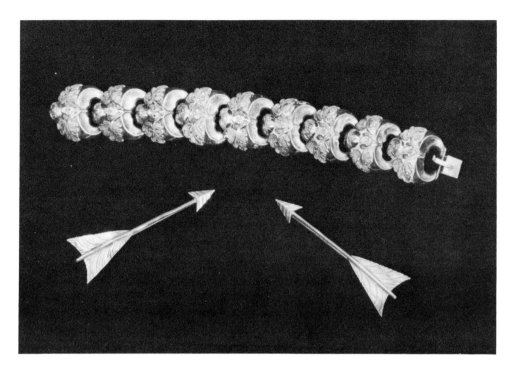

Silver-gilt jewelry, dating from the 1830's. Not intrinsically valuable, but interesting as showing what was worn at that time and because it belonged to a prominent local family.

Silver caster by Benjamin Lord, Rutland, Vermont, 1770–1843. This is the only known piece of hollow ware made by Lord, and the only known piece of Vermont hollow ware made in an eighteenth-century form. *Bennington Museum, Bennington, Vermont.*

to by some as "pleating" or "ruffling"—is popular in old silver. Practically all our early American silver was decorated solely by engraving. This helps distinguish eighteenth-century English from American; during this period much of it looks alike in almost all other respects.

In tankards there are two forms of tops, generally attributed to different areas: Boston silvermakers used a simple flat design; Philadelphians used a raised one, often with turnings and a finial at the top.

Early American silver did not come into its own until the eighteenth century. John Coney of Boston, born in 1655, is one of the earliest recorded makers, and one of the few whose work predated 1700. Paul Revere's father, Apollos Rivoire, came to this country from France, and was apprenticed to Coney, and later passed on his trade to his now famous son. Few realize that Revere worked into the nineteenth century until 1818, at a time when great changes were taking place in silvermaking. Our country had opened up new sources of supplies as an independent nation, and with our growth came a whole new breed of craftsmen who began to turn out great volumes of fine handmade silver. Around 1840, machines took over, and the fine quality and delicate handwork began to disappear.

Pine spoonholder with coin silver spoons, mostly 1810–1830, including one stamped "d. Jarves," possibly by the founder of the Boston and Sandwich Glass Company. Others are by Massachusetts, Connecticut and Rhode Island makers.

In the early part of the nineteenth century, a great deal of what we call "coin silver" was produced. The term "coin" signified that the content was nine parts silver to one part alloy. (Sterling had a 9.25 silver content to .75 alloy content. The word "sterling" was not in general use in this country until about the time of the Civil War.) Because most very thin coin silver spoons are well marked, identification is easy. They are still plentiful, and a good spoonrack full of them is always a pleasure to see and own.

The Boston area produced by far the most early silver. In addition to the Reveres and John Coney, the seventeenth and eighteenth centuries are represented by the following outstanding craftsmen, who created a sufficient quantity to merit looking for their work.

Massachusetts
  Boston: James and Nathaniel Austin, John Ball, Thomas Bentley, John Blowers, John Bridge, Zachariah Brigdon, Samuel Burrill, John Benjamin, William, John, and Samuel Burt, James Butler, John Coburn, William Cowell, Sr. and Jr., Rufus Greene, William Homes, Isaac, Jacob, and Nathaniel Hurd, Joseph Loring, Samuel Minott, David Moseley, Benjamin Pierpoint, William Rouse, William Simpkins, Andrew Tyler, and Edward Winslow
  Salem: John Andrew and John Towzell
  Concord: Nathaniel Bartlett
  Newburyport: Joseph and William Moulton and their sons and grandsons, and Jacob Perkins
  Worcester: Thomas Lynde
Connecticut
  Hartford: Ebeneezer Austin
  Milford: Isaac Beck
  Norwalk: Abel Brewster
  New Haven: Abel Buell and Marcus Merriman
  Fairfield: Nathaniel Burr
  Middletown: William Hardin
  Guilford: Samuel Parmelee and William Ward
Rhode Island
  Newport: Jonathan Otis, Isaac Andrews, Thomas Arnold, and Jonathan Clark
  Providence: Ezekiel Burr and Gideon Casey

New Hampshire
>   Portsmouth: Benjamin Austin, Jedediah Baldwin, William Whit-
>   temore, Samuel and Benjamin Drowne, Timothy Gerrish,
>   John Round, and William Simes

Maine
>   Portland: Eleazor Wyer, Zebulon Smith, John Butler, and Joseph
>   Ingraham

Vermont
>   Rutland, Ludlow, and Woodstock: Roswell H. Bailey
>   Rutland: Bradbury M. Bailey, Frederick Chaffee, and Root Chaf-
>   fee. (Benjamin Lord worked here from about 1797 to 1831,
>   but only one of his pieces has been found. It is the only
>   known piece of hollow ware made in an eighteenth-century
>   form by a Vermont craftsman—a silver caster [page 129] on
>   display at the Bennington Museum.)
>   Montpelier: Ira S. Towne
>   Great Barrington: Jedediah Phelps

All the works produced by these men are wanted by collectors. While the possibility of finding their work is at a minimum, it is possible, and those who are best informed as to the names of makers can make the best buys.

In the early part of the eighteenth century, the English began making Sheffield plate. This was produced by sandwiching a sheet of copper between two sheets of silver under heat and pressure. Less silver content was needed, since these plated sheets could be worked and formed into articles that looked as well as the more solid pieces. Sheffield is marked, and any good guide to maker's marks can help you identify time, maker, and place of origin. A seam was often left when the plate was shaped into a cylindrical form, such as that of a mug or teapot. Most often, this is at the point where the handle was attached, as this would help to hide it. Though the workers also tried to hide the seam by soldering it with pure silver and then hammering and polishing, it may quite often be seen or felt underneath the handle.

In the 1840's, electroplating came into use. Thus items were made directly of copper, brass, white metal, or a combination of them, and could be dipped into a solution that by means of electrolytic action deposited silver on them, covering up soldered joints and seams. Detection is difficult. At last the poor man's silver had arrived, and the production of it was fantastic, hitting its peak at the end of the last century. Most of it is either triple or quadruple plate, meaning it has been dipped three or four times.

Not too long ago formulas were put on the market into which you would dip your silver to clean it instantly. An old wives' method was to put a teaspoon of baking soda in an aluminum washpan and let the silver soak in it a while. These methods worked on the principle of supplying or creating an acid to eat away dirt and tarnish. But a little-known fact is that silver companies, when their products are brand new, will dip them into a compound deliberately to tarnish them. Then they are buffed and polished again, leaving tarnish in the crevices to highlight the designs that have been impressed in them. The companies feel that without this relief, the silver pieces would be too bright and too flat looking, and the designs would lack depth.

There are various opinions about whether worn Sheffield plate should be replated by the dipping process or left with the copper showing through. Some feel that this is the patina of Sheffield and that it should be left alone. Others believe that to restore an old piece to look as it did when it was made originally is acceptable and does not harm its value—rather it will heighten it. Personal taste would seem the best guide.

As far as the electroplated pieces are concerned, replating can only improve their value. Do not hesitate to have it done if you cannot live with the pieces as you find them.

CHAPTER **7**

Dolls and Children's Artifacts

WOODEN penny dolls, made in Germany as far back as the 1400's, began that country's domination of the doll world. Though the French are responsible for some great dolls, especially throughout the nineteenth century, they did not create either the variety or quantity the Germans did. The bulk of those we wish to collect today necessarily come either from France or from Germany.

In this country, the American Indian provided us with clay and wooden dolls. Interesting early American dolls are scarce, and of value to collectors who must have one of everything. Indeed, the best of the dolls made in this country command great prices.

New England, though a prime area of doll collecting, did very little in the manufacture of them. In fact, the country as a whole did not achieve much prominence in dollmaking until after World War I, when imports from Germany and France were curtailed. Our native factories brought out new designs, as well as imitations of imports, and captured the market, never to lose it.

Our earliest native made dolls were of wood, clay, and cloth. These were homemade during the eighteenth century, and those that have survived reveal a variety of artistic talents. Some of them were clothed, and the clothing of some was painted on in crude fashion. Cloth dolls must have been made from scraps of cloth or worn clothing; they sometimes appear grotesque because of the mixing of colors and patterns.

The earliest wax dolls, made in the latter part of the eighteenth century and into the nineteenth, were made by pouring wax into molds, and then painting in the coloring of the mouth, cheeks, and eyes. Later

134

ones were made with a composition base of one kind or another, with the features painted on and then molded over with clear wax. There is one way to tell their approximate age—those made prior to the Civil War had mostly flat-soled shoes painted on; those made after the Civil War had feet with heels molded on. It is difficult to understand why wax dolls were made right up into this century with the more exotic materials available and in general use. Because they were soft, fragile, and quite often damaged, rewaxing was necessary.

During this century, reproductions of earlier wax types were made, and the imitations can confuse one who is not an expert. There are no easy clues for recognizing the older doll. One must gain knowledge by handling them.

Leather dolls came here quite early, too, in the middle of the eighteenth century. These were popular since leather was available in every farm home, and this was a good way to utilize scraps. Faces were painted on. After the Civil War the first patent was taken out to mold dolls' heads from leather. Kid had been popular for hands and legs, and remained so during the entire century. Often, these were purchased all "made up," so that the mother could just stitch them in.

Shortly after Goodyear patented his hard rubber in 1844, rubber dolls appeared in quantity. This was an easily molded, inexpensive material, and could be painted very simply. Soft rubber dolls had been made earlier, but did not survive because of their fragility. The early hard-rubber ones are very desirable, and are often marked with the Goodyear patent name and number.

Celluloid dolls did not appear until the 1880's, yet there are probably more of these dolls than any other kind. They marked the beginning of our great plastics industry of today, and untold numbers of dolls were made in celluloid until right before World War II, when less flammable and less expensive materials were developed. We are all familiar with the celluloid Kewpies—one can only speculate on how many were turned out since their inception in 1913. The first ones were made in bisque; then millions were mass-produced, both in this country and abroad, assuring this doll a place in posterity.

All sorts of metal dolls were made during the last century, including the common tin soldier. Actually, molded metal heads were not popular until after the Civil War, and these were made in Germany. Metal was commonly used for leg and arm joints by then, and unless a doll has been treated with care, these may have rusted. Metal was not so popular as the other materials used, so these dolls were generally of the less expensive variety.

Many dolls had metal in inner working devices to make them perform in some way. The first walking dolls are generally credited to the French, in the early part of the nineteenth century. Some were made in this country as early as 1826. Dolls with primitive talking devices appeared in the 1850's; wetting, 1890's; creeping, 1870's. There was even a doll made in the 1870's that would swim. All these were of French or German manufacture. Earlier than this, of course, simple music boxes were installed inside their bodies to play lullabies or other tunes of the day.

Paper dolls were quite popular as early as the first part of the nineteenth century. The best ones had their clothing and features printed on the back as well as the front. They were dressed in the styles of the day. Paper dolls are still being made. Many of us can remember the funny papers of the thirties when Fritzi Ritz was modeled as a cutout with her wardrobe changing every week, so little sister would see to it that the paper was bought every Sunday. Many were done with the

likenesses of famous actors, actresses, and entertainers. The Jenny Lind paper doll was popular, as well as the Shirley Temple of more recent years.

All this leads to the material used in the first really collectible American dolls—the papier-mâché creations of Ludwig Greiner, patented in 1858. All early doll collectors want at least one Greiner. He was a German immigrant who opened a small toy factory in 1840 in Philadelphia, and turned his talents to dollmaking, creating what some consider the first all-American doll—at least the first one patented in this country. These dolls are fragile, and the features are easily damaged if hit. Greiner's sons carried on his business until the start of this century. They made dolls out of all kinds of materials, but the most valuable are the early papier-mâché. A Greiner must be marked to be accepted as one, for other makers imitated his styles and designs. Of all the Greiners, the 10-inch doll is most sought after.

The center of dollmaking in New England was in a very unlikely place—Springfield, Vermont. One would have expected a more metropolitan area. Joel Ellis opened his factory there right after the Civil War, and began to turn out dolls that are highly prized today. Most

Greiner papier-mâché doll, mid-nineteenth century. *Shelburne Museum, Inc.*

◀

(Left) Edison phonograph doll, 1887–1888, with a china head and tin body, the first talking doll. A wax ribbon record around a metal wheel was inserted in the back. Edison and his men recited nursery rhymes, and the record repeated them. (Center) Set of "Jenny Lind" cutout paper dolls and costumes in the original box; made about 1850. (Right) So-called French fashion doll of about 1869, with bisque head, violet glass eyes, leather arms, and cloth body; pierced ears with earrings.

of these were wooden, and were turned out partly on lathes and partly by a process of steam pressing wood to shape the head and bust section. Ellis had patented his method of fitting the arms and legs into U-shaped slots, where they were simply pinned so they could swing quite freely. During this same period he was responsible for turning out some of the most interesting doll carriages, some with only three wheels. Many have survived because his output was large, but collectors snap them up as quickly as they appear. He gave up dollmaking in 1874 and was replaced immediately by other makers in the same community—most of whom had probably worked for him. Johnson, Taylor, Martin, Sanders, and Mason are some of those associated with this period of manufacture in Springfield.

Another New England manufacturer of note during the latter part of the nineteenth century was the Eclipse Manufacturing Company in Springfield, Massachusetts. They made composition and china-headed dolls that are collectible today.

Patents were issued to such pre-twentieth-century New England doll designers as William Jacques of Newton, Massachusetts, who created a talking doll with a phonograph mechanism and sold the rights to Edison for manufacture, and Henrietta Hinckley in Waterbury and Arthur Hotchkiss of Cheshire, both in Connecticut, for walking dolls. Izannah Walker of Rhode Island patented the famous cloth doll that bears her name.

Probably the country's most important areas of manufacture were New York and Philadelphia. Albert Schoenhut began to manufacture toys and dolls in Philadelphia in 1872. He had the courage to make wooden dolls just prior to World War I. His circus figures, dollhouses, and wooden toys of all types are much in demand today, and they are well marked. Many will be found in New England. Other late nineteenth-century American dollmakers whose works are collectible are Philip Goldsmith Company, Covington, Kentucky; Bisc Novelty Company, East Liverpool, Ohio; and Louis Amberg in New York City. The Fulper Potteries of Flemington, New Jersey, turned out china and bisque heads for dolls at about the time of World War I, and collectors buy them whenever they can.

Throughout this time, imported dolls were greatest in demand because of their appearance and refinements. The fine bisque, china, and Parian heads imported from France and Germany were exquisite.

In addition, foreign makers were well advanced in production techniques, and were still working with nonunion labor, while during our industrial expansion in the nineteenth century wages went up sufficiently to remove us from the competitive market.

Many of the European dolls are well marked for easy identification. If they are not marked, there are some clues for determining age and quality. On the whole, dolls made prior to 1840 had straight hair, either real or painted. After about 1840, until about the time of the Civil War, curly hair was "in." Long curls came in after that time and through the 1870's. During the latter part of the century, short hair was more prevalent. And, as mentioned earlier, the Civil War marks the turning point when the flat-soled foot or shoe went out in favor of those with heels.

Dolls with closed mouths are generally considered of greater value. The style of a doll's clothing can be helpful in pinpointing origin and era. If a doll is of good quality, the head will be finely molded, the coloring will be good, eyes and hair natural in appearance, and extremities well put together, with fine hand stitching evident. Clothing may have been made on a sewing machine, but this does not lower value. Those of interesting or unusual construction, especially those with early

An unusual penny wooden doll, with twin babies, in a ladder-back rocker. *Shelburne Museum, Inc.*

mechanical devices installed, are much in demand. Facial characteristics can be helpful in determining geographic origin.

Very different from the above are dolls handmade at home. It was
quite the fashion for Mother to buy just the head and bust section,
either in china porcelain or Parian, and make up the rest of the doll at
home. If kid feet and hands were not purchased, it is possible for the
doll to have ended up with a simple body stuffed with sawdust, straw,
or cotton. As with other antiques, good workmanship is very important.

Among the more famous French dolls are the Jumeau and the Bru.
These command top prices. In German dolls, look for the K P M,
Königliche Porzellan Manufaktur; S & H, Simon and Halbig; K & K
Toy Company; Kämmer and Reinhardt; and G H, Gebrüder Heubach.
There are many more from each country, but the above are the best,
and may still be found from time to time.

Interesting little dolls like the frozen Charlotte are fairly common
because so many were made. They measure anywhere from three-fourths
of an inch to over a foot. These are fixed figures; their hands and feet do
not move, and they are generally made of bisque. A girl by the name
of Charlotte was immortalized in a poem that tells the story of her
wedding day in Vermont, when she rode from the church in the dead
of winter clad only in her wedding gown, and died of exposure. Some
people call these little fixed dolls "church" dolls, as reputedly they were
given to little girls to keep them occupied during the long hours of
church services, which in very religious communities would last almost
half a day.

Good dolls are still coming out of New England attics, and long-
forgotten trunks house many collectibles. Generally, these are in good
condition, as most were wrapped carefully when they were put away,
and never taken out again by the original owner. Many fine dolls are still
being bought in the ten-to-fifty-dollar price range. Reproductions have
been made, many by the Japanese in their very white bisque, but they
are easy to identify. The rule for marking imports with country of origin
after 1892 makes it easy to identify those made after that time.

We must not forget the contemporary dollmakers whose works are
very much in demand. The late Martha Thompson of Wellesley,
Massachusetts, along with her son Murray, was responsible for many of
the newer fine collectibles. Until her death in 1964, she handmade many
fine specimens, among them the characters from Little Women, and

famous people such as British Royalty, Kate Greenaway figures, and even John and Priscilla Alden.

Gwen Flather of Meredith, New Hampshire, is famous for her cloth dolls, which are marvels of construction. She has modeled many New England characters: among them Robert Frost, an old farmer reading the *Old Farmer's Almanac*, and a sister from the Shaker Colony in Canterbury, New Hampshire.

The State of Maine has contributed Bette Curtis and Jeanne Maker, who are expert in creating dolls in character with the rugged people, past and present, of this fascinating vacation area.

The above people have received national attention, with many of their works exhibited in museums.

A popular slogan during the last part of the nineteenth century was "A penny saved is a penny earned." Possibly as a result, the many clever banks made in tin and iron that were sold throughout the country were tremendously popular. They were good Christmas or birthday gifts, and taught youngsters to save their pennies and have fun doing so.

Small personal savings banks have been with us for centuries. The earliest must have been made from clay in simple pottery forms. Popular during the times of the Pompeians were those made in the shape of fruits, such as apples and pears. These had a slot near the top, and were painted to look like the fruit. These have been dug from ruins, and some returned to this country after World War II with servicemen.

The increased industrial production of our country at the time of the Civil War brought about many new ideas for manufacturers to explore after the war ended. They had plenty of machinery and man-power for peacetime production, and the tin and iron still and mechanical banks were a product of the inventiveness of those times. Perhaps the foremost maker of iron banks was the J. & E. Stevens Company in Cromwell, Connecticut. Others among the ten who made the most and best banks were the Kenton Hardware Company of Kenton, Ohio; the Arcade Manufacturing Company; and Wing, Bliss and Harper.

Many of the banks were designed by individuals who sold their rights to a company for manufacture. Perhaps the most famous was Charles A. Bailey, who did much of the designing for the Stevens firm into the present century. One of his most popular designs was the Teddy and the Bear, a model of Teddy Roosevelt shooting a coin into a tree trunk, at which time a cover snapped back at the top of the trunk just as a bear's head popped out. As an added touch, if a youngster placed a small cap, such as those used in a cap pistol, in the mechanism, it would go off with a bang.

Before the Civil War it was practically impossible for a child to earn money he could call his own. If a child worked, it would be for his parents at no pay, or else he would be apprenticed out where he would work practically for his room and board. With the Industrial Revolution, children were given jobs—sometimes in "sweathouses," and their extra coins would be hoarded in one of the little banks. They were only designed to provide enjoyment while saving, for obviously anyone who chose could steal the bank.

The earlier tin banks were flimsy but interesting. They were held together by bent metal tabs that were molded with the figures they represented. To open a bank, one would have to bend the tabs to dismantle it; and after doing so several times, the tabs were likely to break. A real innovation was the bank made in the shape of a cash register that would total the amount placed in it. At first these registered only one type of coin; later they were refined to include several sizes. Some automatically locked after the first ten cents was put in it, and could not be opened again until a total of ten dollars was deposited. These were made in iron as well as in tin.

Comical figures of the day, comic-strip characters, clowns, trick animals, and comedians were used as models. Some poked fun at ethnic groups; though this was not considered in poor taste at the time, today it affects the resale value of the banks. Many were made in different sizes of the same character—to collect properly one must collect all of them, which is quite a challenge. One wonders how many different banks were made and whether examples of each have turned up in collections, rare as they may be.

A recent auction of still iron banks set some new prices for the rarer items. An analysis of the prices reveals that the figure and animal banks are among the most desired. Such familiar figures as Mulligan the Cop, the Baseball Player, Boy Scout, Buster Brown and his dog Tige, Sharecropper, and Mammy with a Spoon are always in demand. The Rhinoceros, Horse on a Tub, Lion on a Tub, all kinds of dogs, cats, rabbits, horses, and so on are popular. GOP elephants are always good, even if not in an election year. Banks to advertise products were made in the form of refrigerators, stoves, and radios, and many were made in the shapes of autos, trolleys, dirigibles, and ships. Some were made in the shape of the lending institutions themselves, often with a teller seen at a window in front. Some were in the shapes of famous buildings, such as the Woolworth and Flatiron.

In mechanical banks ingenuity was the key to success, and the makers designed figures of animals and people that would respond either in an unusual or in a humorous manner when a coin was inserted: a dentist yanks a tooth from his patient, and the patient falls over backward, much to the delight of children, all for a penny. Jonah is swallowed by the whale; a dog chases a cat up a tree; a bullfrog jumps to grasp a fish that is snatched away just in time by an Indian holding it; a mule kicks a coin into a barn—all these and many more have become rarities in the collecting of mechanical banks. Many of these are being reproduced today, but it is not too difficult to tell the new from the old. Old ones have a look and patina that are acquired only with age.

As for the future, bank collecting is an excellent area in which to interest your children. Many of the still iron banks are relatively inexpensive. And with the interest in the new as well as the old, why not buy the banks put out by our lending institutions today? In time, as these present-day banks disappear and no more are made, they will have to be added to any complete collection; they must therefore rise in value. Because they are made in the shapes of cars, animal forms, Indian heads, and so on, they are the very good collectibles of the not too distant future. Consider a lending institution that may have a thousand penny banks made up as a promotion to introduce new accounts; such banks contain a built-in demand for the future because so few were made and some collectors must have one of everything. Any that are unusual will command greater prices.

Already a mechanical flying-saucer bank that was made in 1956 has risen many times in value. It is an interesting piece of gadgetry that sold originally for only a dollar. So, start your child on bank collecting with a new one on any gift-giving occasion, along with his other presents. When it is time for him to go to college, it is possible that he could pay for his first year by liquidating his collection.

All sorts of old tin and iron toys keep turning up, some of them dating back to post–Civil War days. Favorites were horse-drawn fire engines and wagons, animals on wheels made as pull toys, circus figures, and mechanical games. As with banks, toys of this type made as late as the 1930's are collectible. Sets of electric trains made just before World War II are in demand, and some of the first of the narrow HO train sets have become scarce, as they represent the first of this kind of manufacture. No precise guide can be set forth for collecting items of this type; much has to be left to the whim of the buyer. There is a greater variation in the prices of children's artifacts than in any other area of collecting, and one wonders how dealers price the items. Because it is not common to see two items alike, price comparisons do not help. You must buy emotionally, and hope that what you buy will always be worth at least what you paid for it.

Kate Greenaway was important in the area of children's artifacts. She was at first a designer of Valentine's Day cards, and the little figures she drew in old English costumes had great appeal. She began her work in London during the 1860's by drawing illustrations for books, and broadened her scope to include making designs for Valentines. The children's clothing she sketched was imitated, and much of it was sold as recently as the 1930's in the United States; to be dressed in a Kate Greenaway outfit was the height of fashion. Though she died in 1902, her fame lingered, and there is a cult dedicated to collecting everything related to her. Though much of her work is frothy and based on fantasy, it pictures an untroubled, unhurried era, and nostalgia contributes to the appeal of her artwork.

Old dollhouses and their furniture have almost disappeared from the open market. They must have been costly in their day, and available only to wealthy families, for few crude country-made ones have turned up—or perhaps the survival rate was very low. It is practically impossible to buy a really good old dollhouse in an antique shop. When estates are settled, heirs usually take dollhouses for their own children, leaving few for the open market. Those who deal almost exclusively in dolls and related objects may know where to find a dollhouse, if they do not have what you want in stock, but at a price higher than they wish to invest in it.

Furniture in miniature keeps turning up. Some call such pieces children's toys, while others say they are salesmen's samples. Whatever they are, they have risen in price everywhere. Small chests of drawers, chairs, and desks scaled down for children to use were once made by cabinet-makers who traveled from house to house, turning out furniture on demand, and at the same time making smaller pieces for children in exact proportions to the larger ones. I have seen two Queen Anne highboys that were made thus, and they represent a type of early collectible rarely seen. While one may speculate on the value of some of these pieces, there is no question that some will command prices in ratio to those of their senior counterparts. However, at an auction in New Hampshire in 1968 a perfectly proportioned lift-top pine blanket chest with bootjack feet, eighteen inches long, sold for only $12. Such items, then, are still available at reasonable prices if you wish to collect them.

Though many old children's games can be found, they must be treated as curiosities from the standpoint of collecting. Their values are academic. Though they should be preserved as examples of the eras in which they were made, there is not much money to be made in buying and selling them, nor is there much use in keeping them as an investment.

At shows and flea markets it is interesting to listen to people in their forties exclaim at the fact that toys they played with as children are now selling for many times more than when they were new. Perhaps we should be putting away some Augie Doggies, Mr. Machines, and Barbie dolls for the future.

Victorian dollhouse with furniture of the period. *Bennington Museum, Bennington, Vermont.*

CHAPTER **8**

Oils, Lithographs, and Prints

Oil paintings are the finest collectibles available to the public now. Quality oils can be purchased at relatively low prices, yet they offer the greatest potential for increasing in value. At the same time, they beautify a home as no other wall decoration can.

However, some consider this an unlikely area of collecting because one of normal means can never possess the great paintings of the old masters and must supposedly settle for second and third best. It's true that it is financially impossible today for most of us to buy a Rembrandt or Van Gogh, or even the work of some more recent painters. Monet's painting "La Terrace à Sainte-Adresse" was bought for the Metropolitan Museum of Art in New York for little less than one and one-half million dollars, indicating how a work painted less than a hundred years ago can be valuable indeed. Although most of us will never acquire a work of this caliber, we can see how nowhere else in the art world have prices risen so high. "La Terrace" was bought by the previous owner in 1926 for eleven thousand dollars!

Many fine paintings that were hidden away cause excitement as, one by one, they appear on the open market. And our native tastes and backgrounds help us to appreciate the work of native artists, which tomorrow may be very high in value. As in any other form of collecting, good quality must be sought.

During the eighteenth century and into the first part of the nineteenth, native painters were engaged more in portrait work than in landscapes. As William Hennessey, noted Professor Emeritus at the University of New Hampshire, once said, "The settlers were too busy looking at the soil to look at the scene."

146

In the early days, portrait artists usually went directly to a patron's home and did their work there, generally of every member of the family. Others traveled throughout the countryside during good weather, painting their subjects in return for room and board plus a few extra shillings or dollars. Some saved time by working alone during the winter, painting the bodies of adults and children with nebulous backgrounds, and then, while traveling from home to home in the warmer months, they simply added heads to the previously painted bodies. As a form of mass production, this resulted in many odd and sometimes grotesque pictures that possess quaint charm for collectors. Upon examination of a recently acquired old oil painting, one collector pieced together a very interesting and probable story of a painter who had done a picture of an entire family, including its dog. On his return through the countryside, perhaps a year later, a new baby had arrived in the family, and, as may still be seen, the dog was painted over with the picture of the new arrival. The work of these itinerant painters is readily available, and, as true Americana, they will rise in value as the years pass.

At the other end of the spectrum are the famous portraitists of Boston—John Singleton Copley and John Singer Sargent, who did their work a century apart; Joseph Blackburn of Portsmouth, Robert Feke, James Badger, and James Whistler of Massachusetts. All their work is of museum quality, and not readily available.

New England is still full of the works of artists who worked for many years in the White Mountains of New Hampshire, painting landscapes now prized by collectors. Working in the early part of the nineteenth century, the group known as the White Mountain School included such painters as Alvin Fisher, Jasper Cropsey, and Thomas Doughty; other well-known names were Albert Bierstadt, John Kensett, John Shapleigh, Thomas Cole, George Inness, Asher Durand, and Benjamin Champney. While their works do not command the prices of a Sargent, Copley, or Blackburn, they will soon be out of reach of the modest pocketbook. Many of these landscape artists painted in New York State in the Adirondack, Catskill, and Helderberg mountains, as well as up and down the beautiful Hudson River, and they were identified as members of the Hudson River School. To whichever school you wish to attribute them is a matter for your own judgment. Since many of the same artists worked in both the White Mountains and the Hudson River area, it is difficult to characterize them as members of either school. They were realist painters, and their works have wide appeal

Scene by Thomas Doughty, 1793–1856, one of America's best early landscape artists.

Mount Washington School primitive oil by John Shapleigh, dated 1881; view of Mount Washington from the Ellis River, Jackson, New Hampshire.

because the subjects are recognizable. Albert Bierstadt and Thomas Moran went west, and became famous for their work in the Rockies and Grand Tetons.

Works by the above artists, as well as by many of their contemporaries, are rapidly becoming unavailable to collectors; their works are well documented, for many of them noted the location of the scenes they painted on the backs of the canvases, and they often dated them as well, which adds to their value. Without such documentation a picture has considerably less market worth. Many fine unsigned landscapes turn up for sale, but these must be valued on their artistic merits alone. A fascinating example of an artist whose paintings may be found in New England is Thomas Chambers, who came from England and painted mostly in the Hudson River area from 1830 to 1860. He died in 1866. I have never seen a signed Chambers, yet it is not difficult to recognize one, as his trees and mountains had a beautiful primitive quality not duplicated by any other artist. When compared to his known works, an unsigned oil can safely be attributed to him, but without documentation the price is held down. Since so little has been discovered about Chambers, one critic has even suggested that he never really existed and that all paintings done in this primitive style are automatically attributed to this name.

Not all artists used canvas. John Burgham of Concord, New Hampshire, painted the wooden panels of the famous Concord stagecoaches that helped conquer the West. He painted native mountain scenes, which gave the coaches an elegant look. Some of these panels have survived. Other artists painted on slabs of native granite, on sea shells, lampshades, and furniture. Thomas Hill and his brother John, who came from England, were at first employed in Wakefield, Massachusetts, decorating chairs with paintings. Some of these were signed.

Gradually, as the White Mountains became known as an ideal place to spend a summer vacation, and as the new railroads encouraged the building of huge hotels near mountains, lakes, and rivers, tourists came from as far away as the Midwest to escape the heat, and the wealthy would stay for the entire summer. The artists profited. In the spring they would pack their easels and head north. Until the tourists arrived, they would paint favorite scenes, among them, Mount Washington, from many different vantage points. During the summer, the artists set up their studios, put their efforts on display, and took orders. During the fall and winter months they retired to their studios, made as many copies as ordered, and sent them by mail to all parts of the country. That is why so many fine landscapes of the New England area may be found even beyond the Mississippi.

Despite lack of documentation, landscapes of good quality that were done during the nineteenth century and even into the early part of this century represent a collectible that will rise in value. Condition is important. Though there are artisans who make a specialty of cleaning and restoring oils, this can be costly. Expensive restoration should be reserved for signed pieces that already have value.

Proper frames are important. Gilded, highly ornamented frames are in keeping with the period. These are basically frames of pinewood with decorations of plaster of Paris molded to them. Spraying with a gold spray is often enough to restore them, as long as they are not damaged.

If a frame is severely damaged, you should soak the frame in water to loosen the plaster decorations; scrape and sand down the wooden frame beneath; and then scrub it with muriatic acid to remove the embedded whiteness. Take care to protect your hands with rubber gloves. Then, simply polish the frame with a good heavy wax or refinish it with clear stain varnish. Most of these frames are of the curved ogee shape, and turn out beautifully, as the wood has aged beneath the plaster and the soft patina will give it excellent quality.

While many artists were busy painting scenes on land, there were an equal number painting sea scenes. Marine paintings are much in demand, and the supply is getting smaller. Those that show the American flag flying are worth more than those with flags of other nations. Unfortunately, flags may have been changed by a clever artist. If you buy a painting that has been altered in this manner, its resale value may be less. When buying fine oils it is best to consult reputable people to appraise them. Paintings of sailing vessels are very good, and those with men on board performing their duties are more valuable. Because merchant ships often flew the flag of the company that owned them, identification may be made from old records of the history of the ship.

All pictures of American ships may not have been painted in American waters by native artists. There is great interest in collecting those that were painted in foreign ports, especially in the Orient. When an American schooner dropped anchor in a harbor, a painter might quickly do a painting of it and offer it for sale to the captain. Many captains brought such paintings home, and occasionally they appear for sale. New England has several excellent marine museums that feature such paintings, along with other seafaring artifacts. These are in Mystic, Connecticut, New Bedford and Salem, Massachusetts, and Bath, Maine. Whatever you pay for paintings on a par with those in these museums, it is fairly certain they will all increase in value as the years go by. They are a very good investment.

In New England, one must use good judgment when buying a painting signed by T. Bailey. He is supposed to have painted on the North Shore above Boston, and was famous for his marines. It is also said that since he was an immigrant, he Anglicized his name to make it more acceptable to his Yankee patrons, and proceeded to turn out a voluminous amount of work. Research has shown that at least five painters signed their works with this name, and perhaps untold others that were never recorded did so too. It appears that such a man did exist and that he had many students, who perhaps went on painting after leaving his studio, signing their works, as they had in the past, with the master's name. This has made great art galleries uneasy, and recently they have begun reclassifying some of their treasures. When buying a T. Bailey picture, its value should be judged on quality alone, rather than on the name attached to it. Some of the work, I feel, is quite poor.

We should not overlook the work of our contemporary artists. Art centers have been set up all over the country, and New England has its share. Country fairs have expanded their showings of native talent; the outstanding one in this respect is sponsored by the Rochester Agricultural and Mechanical Association in New Hampshire, which holds its annual fair about the third week in September. This has grown to a showing of about four hundred oils, entered from all over New England, and it has been necessary to build a complete exhibition gallery to house them. Most are for sale. Antique shows and flea markets are attracting dealers who exhibit nothing but paintings.

The paintings of today are the antiques of the future, and local artists are turning out quality work. Ribbons at shows and exhibitions will tell what is the best in the opinion of judges. Combine their confidence in the painters with your own appraisal, and make your decision.

Of great value someday will be pictures of noted public buildings that may disappear under urban-renewal programs: bridges, town squares that will someday suffer modernization; quaint fishing villages; landscapes that may be changed by housing or commercial developments; and contemporary scenes and the artifacts that surround us. Buying still lifes, a picture of an old, unidentified barn, or a road in autumn with trees ablaze in color may bring you pleasure, but they may not result in any growth in the value of your investment. People will still be able to paint such scenes fifty years from now. Of course, if you are lucky and happen to buy the paintings of someone who may reach great heights in the art world, anything you own by that artist would be good—but this is a long chance.

A word of warning: With the scarcity of the works of older, reputable artists, we have seen the growth of promotions to sell the public on a particular painter. When an estate is settled, a collection of paintings done by the master or mistress of the house or some distant relative may come to light. A favorite ploy is to draw up a catalogue of such works and to arrange an exhibition of them. With such attention paid to unimportant "art," it is no wonder that some buyers pay good money for mediocre work, hoping they are "getting in on the ground floor" with the canvases of someone who may be famous someday. Most of them, however, never are.

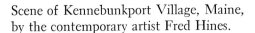

Scene of Kennebunkport Village, Maine,
by the contemporary artist Fred Hines.

Among the rarer forms of reproduction is the woodcut. A Bostonian, John Foster, is credited with doing the first woodcut in this country—that of the likeness of the Reverend Richard Mather in 1670. This was not a new technique; it had been used before the days of Johannes Gutenberg, who was born around 1400. Until he invented movable type, all printing was done by carving a wooden block to reproduce an entire page at a time. Carvers are still busy with this trade today, turning out contemporary prints. Some command high prices, and are being shown in museums and galleries. There are still good old woodcut prints to be collected, and those by Timothy Cole and Thomas Bewick are to be sought. This technique died out as soapstone and steel engravings came in, so there is not too much available.

Also rare is line engraving, which was done on copper. Even Paul Revere tried his hand at it. Ink is rubbed over the engraving, and then wiped clean, leaving just the ink that has settled into the cut—then a paper is rolled over it, under pressure, allowing it to soak up the ink, and creating the picture.

Perhaps the rarest form of engraving is the mezzotint, because it is so difficult to execute. Though this work is being done today, the early mezzotints of quality are hard to come by. Yet, when they are found they do not bring a great price, as there is little demand for them. Mezzotints were made as early as the seventeenth century. A copper plate is first roughed up by lightly scratching its entire surface; then the desired picture is worked into it, with the roughened areas smoothed down and shaded so that when inked and reprinted, variations of color or black and white would occur. The result was more like a painting than like a line engraving that reproduced no shaded colors. Peter Pelham of Boston, who worked in the eighteenth century, was our first mezzotint artist.

Etching differs from the above processes. An acid-resistant coating is applied to a copper plate; the artist then cuts his picture through the coating to the copper below. Nitric acid is then applied, eating into the etched areas without harming the remaining coated areas.

Lithography is an entirely different process. Water- and paint-repellent substances are rolled alternately on a soapstone. The design is first drawn on the stone with a water-repellent wash. Then water is spread on, soaking into the untreated areas so that when the lithograph ink is applied it will rest only on those areas where the water has been repelled.

The printing is then done, with the ink adhering to the surfaces of the design, and being repelled from the other areas.

Most lithography was done outside New England, though many New England scenes were reproduced. Perhaps most prolific was the firm of Nathaniel Currier and J. M. Ives, whose work spanned the years between 1835 and the 1890's. Though they worked in New York, they were the lithographers to the nation. Their work was tremendously popular, and they turned out prodigious numbers of prints dealing with our wars, life in the country, celebrations, great events, scenic views, animals, birds, marine life, political, social, and sporting events. The best values in lithographs are those that depict famous places and people. Good marine lithographs, and scenes of harbors and communities as they looked many years ago, are always good, and the firm of Currier and Ives, along with many contemporaries, filled countless homes in New England with their huge output. Though some of these prints may be had today for a few dollars, some rise into four figures, indicating that age and the maker's name alone do not explain value; the subject matter counts. American prints are more desired than European ones. Because scenes of famous cathedrals in France or castles in England have limited

Lithograph, "George Washington and His Generals."

value in the United States, collect those of political, scenic, or historic importance in this country. However, in sections of our country where people are more oriented to European designs and craftsmanship, foreign lithographs assume greater importance, and your best buys in these will be found in New England, since they are not in local demand.

To see artists in museums making copies of the oils hanging in the galleries can make the new collector a little nervous. He may well wonder how much of this was done in the past to cloud the authenticity of works bought today. But there is a rule against reproducing the picture in the exact dimensions used by the original artist, and since all recognized works are immediately catalogued once they come to light, any discrepancy in dimension would be noted. Exact copies that may have been done in the past may be detected by analyzing scrapings of the paint to determine age. It is advisable to seek competent advice when investing a great deal of money in oils.

One of the most difficult things to recognize as not being of the best quality is a lithograph done on canvas. These look like oil paintings, yet they are not, and one must be sure he is paying an appropriate price. This technique was used mostly on large reproductions of paintings. A person not able to afford a large oil might settle for the lithograph, while a small oil was generally within the reach of the casual buyer. This technique is used today to make the large reproductions of pictures that are to be found in department stores. Works of Matisse, Picasso, Soyer, Amen, and a host of other artists are being reproduced everywhere; they can be stamped out at will to fill the demand. If you wish this type of reproduction, buy them. They are decorative, and most are well framed. But one must judge the cost of these against the cost of true one-of-a-kind oil paintings by contemporary artists, which are bound to rise in value so long as the work is good.

CHAPTER 9

Other Collectible Items

THERE are antique collectibles to be found in New England that do not fit into neat categories. Many of these border on being antiques, while some are just collectibles, an interesting part of our heritage.

Lighting devices are a fascinating area. About the only requirements for an early lamp were a font in which oil or other melted fat could be stored and a wick to absorb the oil to feed the flame. Apparently animal fats were first used, giving way in later years to olive oil, whale oil, from which wax for candles was made, and petroleum, as well as kerosene and other, more exotic, fuels. Despite our technological advances made in so many other areas, lighting improvement was comparatively slow in the United States. As recently as the 1930's, many youngsters were still studying their school lessons by oil lamp or candles.

Candles came into general use in the sixteenth and seventeenth centuries. All sorts of devices to hold them were turned out by clever craftsmen. Their designs were so classic that the candleholders we buy today are made in exactly the same fashion as those of this early period. Flemish and English designs are copied faithfully—it is difficult sometimes to tell the old from the new, once a patina has been acquired. To be sure of the age of a candleholder, one must look at the bottom of it to see the manner in which it is finished. Some are held together by old hand-cut brass nuts; others are crudely soldered together, and many had the push-up stem that allowed one to remove the stub of the candle once it had burned down to the holder. Newer ones are machine-finished, and show no signs of this earlier work.

During this period of elegant brass and silver holders, country people contented themselves with the crudest forms of oil lamps and candle-holders. Oil lamps were simple iron pans that held some sort of oil or grease and from the four corners of which hung rag wicks. Then there was the familiar Betty, or crusie, lamp, which is made of iron and is attached to a hanger so the light may be taken anywhere and hung where needed. The pans that hold the oil are almost pear-shaped, with the wick at the narrowest point. Some are built double, one above the other. This is sometimes called a double lamp with two wicks, while others say the bottom pan was placed to catch the drippings as the oil burned in the wick above. Both explanations make sense, and perhaps they were used in both ways.

Primitive candleholders made of iron could be hung from adjustable ratchet hangers or stuck in a block of wood to serve as a table light. Some of these were made with a rush holder that could be used to supplement the light of the candle.

While iron grease lamps survive today as curiosities, candleholders are still in widespread use. More candles are being used today per capita than at any time in our past. Candle shops have sprung up everywhere. While the purpose of candles used to be utility, today design, scent, and

Unusual seventeenth-century brass candle-holder. *Shelburne Museum, Inc.*

Miniature oil lamps, nineteenth century.
Mrs. E. J. Delmore Collection.

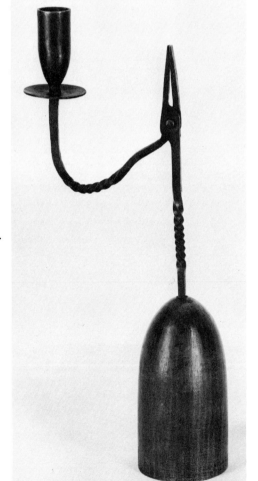

Wrought-iron candle and rush holder.
Shelburne Museum, Inc.

color seem to be ruling factors. Eating by candlelight is a gracious amenity, and almost every restaurant designed with a colonial or country influence has candles at each table.

Amazingly enough, more of the world is still lighted by oil and paraffin than by electricity or gas. There are many underdeveloped nations where people live just as their forefathers did. For this reason, if you wish to collect early lighting devices, you may look to these countries for an excellent supply. New England has its share, but the older ones are fast disappearing. The most exotic lighting devices were made overseas, and various designs from different countries will add interest to any collection.

In the 1820's we went into the "whale oil" period, which lasted until the 1840's, when coal oil and finally kerosene held sway. Whale-oil lamps are relatively plentiful in New England, as the great seaports from which the whaling schooners sailed were close by. Most lamps were turned out in glass or tin; some were made in pewter, and fewer in brass. The lamps had two spouts at the top that held round wicks but no chimney. As a result they smoked while burning, making the chimney-equipped kerosene oil lamps a welcome replacement. The lamps that look like whale-oil lamps but have two much longer spouts and wicks were designed to burn camphene, a very volatile mixture of alcohol and turpentine that burned with a clear flame and little or no smoke. The longer spout wick was designed to keep the flame as far away from the storage font as possible, as the camphene was known to explode if overheated. There were many fires because people carelessly burned camphene in the shorter whale-oil lamps.

Kerosene lamps are still with us today. Practically every farm home or summer cottage in New England is equipped with them—some old, some new. They provide quick emergency light when needed. Older ones are finding their way into the antique market as owners find they can be sold at a relatively good sum and replaced at much less cost with a new one. New England is an excellent region to buy old oil lamps, since the products of New England glassmakers are more plentiful locally. Because of the beautiful colorings and designs of this glass, all serious collectors scour the countryside for them.

New England is also a good area to find miniature oil lamps. Most of these stand less than eight inches in height, and were used primarily as night-lights in children's rooms. Some burned medicinal oils and some were used as vaporizers in sickrooms. Though most were American made, there were some imports. Some are made in Amberina, Peachblow, Quilted Satin, and other exotic glasses, and are often collected by glass collectors as well as lamp collectors.

The Gone with the Wind lamp is a misnomer that resulted from a mistake made by Hollywood set designers. In many scenes the film featured the now familiar lamp with the large round base and large round globe with a chimney poking through it. Because the story took place at the time of the Civil War, historians were amused—since these lamps did not make their appearance until the 1880's. However, the name became a convenient means of identifying them. These were made in a miniature size, too.

There must be thousands of Portland glass lamps, unmarked and unidentified, in Maine as well as the rest of New England. Portland's main product was lamps, and they were shipped all over the world. Those with colored shades and known designs may be traced to Portland manufacture, but most of these were taken out of circulation long ago. Country auctions in Maine are the best place to look for them. Check the patterns at the Portland Museum of Art, then go and buy.

Frosted-leaf decorated shade lamp, Portland glass, circa 1836–1873. *Portland, Maine, Museum of Art.*

Collecting old books makes sense if you can use them. Some decorators buy old leather-bound books, without caring about their contents, to dress up bookcases and tables. Why not collect good ones? For interest, pleasure, and financial rewards the best books to collect are town, country, and state histories. These are largely available, and most of them are not yet prohibitively expensive. They are excellent for teaching children their local heritage. Writers use them for research, and lawyers find them invaluable when checking into the history of properties and the families who owned them. Most towns had biographers, and there were many such writers who were busy during the latter part of the last century. These old books are being updated today, and these should be collected as well. Look for those that deal with your area and state, where they will be most valuable. The best place to buy many of these books is a nearby state, whose residents have no interest in what happened in yours, and therefore prices are down. Genealogies, biographies of famous men and state atlases are very good. In this way some people have begun a profitable career of writing for local newspapers, which are always interested in occurrences of the past.

Though old documents and deeds fall into this same category, they are not worth as much. Their basic value is to occupants of properties who would like to preserve anything historical about the place in which they live. Old store ledgers are only curiosity pieces. Military commissions signed by famous people are very good, but it is the signature that has the value, not the document. Autograph books containing names of important people appeal to many collectors. Christmas, Valentine, and ordinary post cards are judged by their age and the work on them. Nuances in values are interesting; there are such simple rules as the fact that a standing Santa is worth more than a sitting one because fewer were made. Old Bibles are almost valueless because so many millions were printed. Though any Bible predating 1800 would be of interest, it would still be limited in value. Early hand-set Bibles, or those from the primitive printing presses of the pre-1700 era, are the ones that command a good price. Any appraisal of the above items must be done on the basis of what others like them have sold for—or by the more hazardous means of paying what something is worth to you. There is no easy way to catalogue documents and books when they are one of a kind; they must be bought and sold on the basis of emotion alone.

One area of book collecting that holds great promise is that of books on antiques. Many limited editions of books that have been privately printed contain very worthwhile information on a variety of subjects. Perhaps a serious collector assembled pictures of his possessions and wrote down all he knew about them. Because general publishers found the work lacked appeal from the standpoint of sale to the general public, the owner would then pay to have them printed and simply give them away to friends and libraries so his efforts would not be wasted. Among such are the three excellent books and two pamphlets done by Philip Hammerslough on his collection of early American silver at the Wadsworth Atheneum in Hartford. Three hundred copies of volumes 1 and 2 were printed, along with 250 copies of Volume 3, as well as similar limited printings of the pamphlets. There is a great demand for these outstanding and scarce books.

Our Pioneer Potters is the title of another rare book, written by Arthur W. Clement of Brooklyn. It covers the early work of potters in this country, and contains more information on little-known or unheard-of men than any other publication, yet only five hundred copies were printed in 1947. Try locating Carl Dreppard's *Old American Prints, The Old China Book,* the story of Samuel McIntire by N. Hudson Moore, or *The Woodcarver of Salem* by Frank Cousins and Phil M. Riley. These are only a few of many that are sought by collectors. The book of today in a limited edition, especially privately printed ones, may well be very collectible tomorrow.

Collections of antique magazines have been sold for great sums, so keep those that you receive each month. Save commemorative booklets that are often published in conjunction with important events in your community. Because they picture your hometown as it is now, they will be enjoyed fifty years from now just as you enjoy looking at pictures from the past. I have seen collections of good-conduct and merit-achievement tokens that were given to children over a hundred years ago, in schools; I have also seen a quaint old dance card that states, "Ladies are not permitted to flirt with the gentlemen." Though old advertising literature, books on medicines, and signs and posters are of interest, they are limited in value.

Old photographs, daguerreotypes, and tintypes are plentiful, but unless they are of famous people they haven't much value. Stereoscopic viewers and the double picture cards that are used with them have experienced a renaissance in value. Many of the simple hand-held stereopticons, as well as their cards, are to be found in New England. The automatic ones that rested atop a table and changed cards as they were cranked or otherwise motivated are not readily available, however. Many were made in this country and many in Europe, but collectors have just about exhausted the supply in New England. The cards are plentiful, as most of them were made in northern New Hampshire. Photographers were employed all over the world to record sights and scenes during the latter part of the first decade of the twentieth century. This was the TV of our grandfathers' day, and was the first practical use of three-dimensional viewing.

The floors in our earliest homes were either sand or wood, or wood covered with sand. The sand was swept out from time to time, and replaced. Even when wood floors became common, it was a rarity to see any sort of floor covering on them in the 1600's. Perhaps the earliest coverings appeared at the beginning of the eighteenth century, and then only in the homes of the wealthy.

Animal skins were used on the floors of log cabins and country homes. These were gradually replaced with common rag rugs made from remnants of old clothing and linens. At first these were made by sewing patches of material together after overlapping them, creating what are often called "tongue rugs," because the pieces were most often rounded. These were followed by patch rugs, which were made by sewing scraps to a backing, creating a design with different colors. Next came the braided rug, and then the hooked rug, which was made by sewing strips or yarns to a backing. Sentiment was often attached to these, for women quite often used clothing of members of their family to make the rug, which they would then keep in the family as a memento. Old tufted rugs, more a product of the South, will not be found in New England. Large embroidered rugs may be the result of up to four or five years of work, and naturally these are highly prized, and therefore scarce.

Practically all the hooked and braided rugs that are so plentiful in New England were made in this century. Older ones were either worn beyond usage or kept in cedar or blanket chests and handed down to members of the family. Though these do appear at estate auctions from time to time, they are high in price. Many people still make these rugs, and country fairs are full of examples of their work. Documenting the age on a braided or hooked rug can be next to impossible once it acquires a worn look. Pay what you want for a rug, based on your desire and need.

Oriental rugs came to this country in the eighteenth century on the clipper ships. Some were from China and Japan, and of course many came from the Near East. These are made by a time-consuming hand-knotting process. This type of work was done in areas from the Balkans to China, and it may be difficult to determine country of origin unless the rug is marked. The wool from sheep and goats was dyed with natural colorings from plants and roots, but for one color, oxblood, the actual blood of the animal was used. Today, synthetic dyes are commonly used, and it would be difficult to tell them from the original ones. Oriental rug sizes are identified by name, such as Qali, which would be about a 6 x 10 or over, and Kellegi, which is a rug usually two or three times longer than it is wide. A Kenareh is a runner that may be up to twenty feet long and approximately a yard wide. Many designs are named after the communities or countries in which they are made. Iran, alone, has given us the names of Ardabil, Bijar, Hamadan, and Mehriban, along with many others. Dealers can recognize the village of origin from patterns and colors, but this is a study that takes years. The novice buyer would do well to consult with dealers in this field. If you are at an auction and you must make a hasty decision for one you like, ask the auctioneer his advice at the time of the inspection or sale.

Since Oriental rugs are all handmade, and the cost of hand labor is up in the rapidly developing nations, some of those made just after World War II are commanding better prices than old ones. These rugs are a good investment in quality and beauty as well as money. They have been imitated by carpetmakers in this country and Europe, notably Belgium. But these are most often shoddy imitations that wear out easily. Some fine ones in Oriental designs have been made in this country with heavy backings. The weight of them will tell their quality, as well as their condition after wear. Though they are serviceable, do not invest money in them, hoping that they will grow in value.

If you are restoring an old home, all these rugs are very much in keeping with the early history of our country. But because a fine Oriental rug will often overshadow the furniture in a room, consider this factor if you wish to emphasize your furniture.

Not many old bed coverings have survived the eighteenth century. Because the settlers raised their own flax and sheared their own sheep, they had fibers to use for spinning on either the low wheel or the tall wheel. Irish immigrants who came to Derry, New Hampshire, are credited with bringing the first small wheels with them. These stand less than three feet high, and are powered by a foot treadle. While the tall, or spinning, wheel, as many call it, can be used only for the spinning of wool, the small wheel could spin just about any fiber. The old linsey-woolseys are perhaps the most desired of any of the old bed coverings. These are double layered, with a different color on either side. Their name suggests they have been made of a mixture of linen and wool, but some people maintain they are wool alone. Even moth-eaten ones bring good prices.

Next in importance are the figured quilts and coverlets. Most of these are pieced or appliqué. The pieced ones were made of separate pieces of cloth sewed together. The appliquéd ones were made by sewing the pieces to a backing. Designs are important, as well as colors. Even the dated ones are very good if they are old. Sometimes friendship quilts were made up of squares, each square fashioned by a different person and then sewn together. They may also have been made as wedding presents or as items made by churchwomen to be raffled at church fairs. Some of these are excellent examples of folk art. The ordinary patch-

Alphabet monogram quilt, with seven other alphabets in script, block, and old English. Featured are colors of the rainbow. *Shelburne Museum, Inc.*

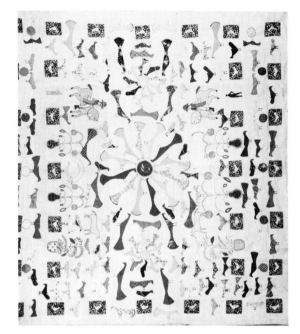

Late eighteenth-century counterpane, linen, in natural color, with motifs of different birds and animals. Appliqué, chainette and chain stitch.

Deer and eagle coverlet of red wool, 92 inches by 80 inches. Begun in 1831, it was finished in 1851. Red predominates on one side, white on the other. *Shelburne Museum, Inc.*

work and simple log-cabin design quilts are relatively inexpensive today. But it will be a very long time before they rise much in value.

Crewelwork and needlework are plentiful, as almost all homes are equipped with linens. Again, condition, color, and design are important. Much of this deserves to be sold individually—some by the boxful. Since there is no shortage, and price should not be a barrier, wait until you find what you want.

Occasionally an outside factor will influence the purchase price. Not long ago an estate was settled that was owned by the former owners of a woolen mill that had made excellent wool blankets for many years. These had long been off the market, but in the estate were many new ones that had been carefully stored and were in perfect condition. The elegance of the blankets, plus the sentiment attached to them in the community, produced prices far above the cost of similar new merchandise at that time.

New England is abundant with samplers, which every girl, generally between the ages of ten and fourteen, had to make. These were most often an exercise in needlework, done in letters of the alphabet, numerals, and local scenes. The dated ones are best, and those of the eighteenth century are scarce. Kits for doing this type of work are being sold today, and some of the newer creations are appearing in shops. Since they are handwork, they have value if they have been done well.

If you collect fans, you must go to metropolitan areas. The fans you will find in the countryside are mostly advertising-card fans that were given out by commercial concerns. As a boy, I remember going to the town hall to see traveling vaudeville and Chautauqua groups, and cardboard fans were always passed out on hot nights—the gift of some local store or wholesaler. These are colorful, and contain all sorts of information—recipes, train schedules, horoscopes, and so on. These are very "camp," and can provide effective decoration in the proper surroundings.

Fine silk, ivory, and sandalwood fans, however, rarely found their way to the poorer country homes. Ladies of fashion lived in the cities, and they always carried fans to important events, even if it was cold outside. Cigars of years ago were not so fragrant as are those of today, and fans helped keep the air moving. Also, there were small mirror fans that enabled a woman to keep an eye on her husband—or on someone else's. The best fans to collect are the carved ivory ones, which came mostly from the Orient, and the silk fans, which came mostly from France. Many of the silk ones are hand-painted with scenic views and genre motifs. These are very good. Decorators may frame them or hang them individually as wall decorations. They are very effective, and an inexpensive replacement for smaller oil paintings. Many other materials were used in their manufacture, including leather and tortoiseshell. Fans are relatively inexpensive because there are few collectors. However, fine ones aren't plentiful, and New England is not the best area for them.

No house is liquidated without producing a box or jar of old buttons. Collectors like good carved ones in wood or ivory—also early brass ones, especially military. Buttons must have been made out of just about every natural or synthetic product ever invented. I've seen them in bone, Bakelite, hard rubber of the mid-nineteenth century, tortoiseshell, glass, china, porcelain, gold, silver, and other metals, as well as some woven from hair, silk, or other fibers. Some of these command good prices, but this is another area where the best rarely rise into three figures. Age and design help to determine value.

Old firearms dating back to the Revolutionary War keep turning up. Most plentiful of the military weapons are those of the Civil War, though prices are up. Old Winchesters, Smith and Wessons, and Colts are not plentiful in New England; most of these went west. Many of the Springfields were made at the Springfield Armory in Massachusetts —they were relatively plentiful and many returned home with servicemen to this area. Eli Whitney not only invented the cotton gin but also, in Connecticut, made some of the finest of early firearms. During Jefferson's administration, Whitney turned out over 40,000 pieces for the government. He also made many for Samuel Colt, whose plant burned down in 1843. Whitney is credited with making the first hammerless rifle in 1866. His arms turn up from time to time, but are scarce. Not too many years ago it was almost impossible to sell any shotgun with the twist spring steel or Damascus barrel. These were made for black powder, and were not safe to use with the newly developed smokeless powders. These are coming into their own as collectors' items now, and any made by the really fine makers, like Parker, Fox, and Lefever, are of value.

There were many fine local gunsmiths, but their works have been pretty much bought up by people in their respective areas. Some of the most successful collectors of these are women who, when on social visits, often find old family pieces.

Guns of the Spanish-American War, especially those of .45 to .70 caliber, are the last of the really old guns that are collectible. Those made in this century have not changed much in function, concept, or design. New materials, such as nylon for barrel and epoxies for stocks, have appeared but are not well accepted. A good sportsman likes the feel of finely etched steel and wood in his hands. The synthetics should soon disappear, only to become curiosity pieces years from now—collected avidly by future antiquers as interesting examples of this period. World War I and II weapons are not antiques, but they are plentiful in New England and are included in good collections of military weapons.

Old powder horns, especially those that have scrimshaw on them and are named and dated, are very good. Shot pouches in leather, copper, brass, or tin are valued according to age and condition. These are relatively plentiful, and prices are not yet exorbitant.

Be careful when you buy swords. Many are merely ceremonial and their values academic. Swords of Civil War vintage and earlier are good. Insist on documentation, unless such is inscribed on it. Wooden canteens of the Revolutionary War are in surprisingly good condition when found. Wooden ones were also used in the Civil War. The Union forces for the most part had tin canteens, and those with an eagle impressed in the sides are very desirable. After the war, some of these were misused. I have seen a popcorn popper that was made by splitting such a canteen in half, with a handle and screened top attached to one of the halves.

With the rise in interest in Mediterranean styles for furniture and other decorations, old armor and related objects have come into their own. The Schuller Museum in New Hampshire has an outstanding collection. Fine suits of armor have risen into the six-figure category. The 1969 Sears catalogue lists a suit of armor for $1,500, intended to attract a frustrated decorator who must have such a figure to complete a medieval setting properly. Though suits of mail, broadswords, lances, and shields are very decorative, they are almost impossible to acquire.

CHAPTER **10**

Tips on Buying Antiques

A SHORT time ago, in a nationally distributed antique magazine, there appeared an ad listing "15 different pieces of barbed wire, only $7.50," followed by the name and address of the enthusiastic advertiser. Nearby were two other ads for the same commodity. One dealer asked, "Are these people knowledgeable or crazy?" Who knows what may be tomorrow's treasure?

There is much to be said about the preservation of our past way of life. Museums and restorations of entire villages have been set up at great expense to do so. Curators search continually for unusual items that were used by our forefathers in order to learn as much as possible about the days gone by.

The collector of the unusual is always welcome at auctions and antique shops. He can be counted on to buy items other people wouldn't take as gifts. In the early 1950's I recall selling leaded-glass and oyster-shell lamps, and hearing people remark, "What are they going to do with that junk?" Today, some of these pieces are valued in three figures.

Tiffany vases that once sold for two or three dollars at auction are bringing two or three hundred now. Carnival glass, orange iridescent that was given away as prizes at fairs just a short time ago, used to sell for twenty-five cents a box. Today that is the minimum price for a single item, and some pieces sell for many dollars.

People collect buttons, paperweights, manhole covers, empty beer cans, and all sorts of trivia. They do so only to satisfy the urge to collect and to become an expert on something from the past. I do not recommend this type of collecting for young marrieds who are truly interested in antiques. It would be more sensible for them to collect a variety of items that are usable. Why not collect tables, chairs, chests of drawers, beds, china, glass, silver, and other household necessities that can still be used? New merchandise that is later resold loses value. If you buy antiques—many still cost less than good reproductions—you will find dealers ready and willing, in a few years, to offer a profit.

In the field of antiques, a little knowledge can be more dangerous than none at all. One who knows a little can have greater problems than the one who knows nothing and relies on the good advice and judgment of reputable dealers and auctioneers.

Some people mistakenly consider almost anything old an antique. Basically, an antique must be an object that is either wholly or partly handmade; it must also be of good quality, taste, design, and construction. Age gives it value, and scarcity heightens its desirability. Many of the items people buy are collectibles, but they are not antiques. A collectible is something from the past that is looked on as an oddity or as a beautiful piece, even though it may have been made by a machine.

Some collectors become experts in the history of their particular field of interest, and are sought as lecturers by historical societies and organizations. Others appear on television, are interviewed by newspapers, and write books. Some become officers or directors of clubs that are formed to attract others to the art of collecting, and such leadership could lead to traveling around the country, making new friends, and collecting interesting antiques, a suitable prospect for retired couples.

As for what to collect, shops and auctions have, at low prices, bottles, bells, buttons, fans, jewelry, all sorts of pottery, pattern glass, old books, primitive oils, early tools, and many other items. Any type of early manufacture native to your hometown area is good to collect, such as pottery, glass, or iron. These have native significance, as well as warmth and charm, and make wonderful conversation pieces.

Collectors should read continually. There are many fine books that will make your hobby more fun and worthwhile. Join a club whose members have the same interests that you do, and you can learn much by profiting from other people's mistakes. You will quite easily become knowledgeable.

One day a lady who had a loom to sell called me. It was set up in her attic. "I have to be out by this Saturday," she said, "and I'd like to have you come and buy it right away." She soon learned some of the facts of "antique life." We may marvel at interesting old artifacts in museums and restorations, yet if anyone offered them to us, we would decline, not having the space to store them or the desire to own them. Though museums and restorations display unusual pieces, they do so in order to show people, to the fullest extent possible, the exact living conditions of years ago. Such items are on display more for their aesthetic than for their monetary value. In addition, most museums and restorations have limited funds, as most are nonprofit, and they prefer items on a donation basis. Besides, by now most museums and restorations are well stocked with looms.

A collector who buys a cumbersome loom in an attic must spend a whole day dismantling it, moving it, and reassembling it in his shop, where it takes up a lot of space while patiently waiting for a customer. This time and money spent could have been invested in a more desirable item.

Even small collectibles, while interesting, may bring little money. Recently, one of our first electric frying pans (it was never used and was made by a nationally known concern) sold for only three dollars at an auction. The early sewing machines of Elias Howe, still in working condition, rarely bring over five dollars. There are many types of wagons and sleighs that sell for a minimal price. Monstrosities of the Victorian and later eras—umbrella stands, combination bookcase-china cupboards, cemetery urns, and so on—are laughed at when they appear. Though corn shellers, bean winnowing machines, hay cutters, cheese presses, winepresses, butter workers, pea shellers, harness vises, wagon jacks, and other paraphernalia found about a farm are interesting, they generally sell for very little when auctioned.

The next time you call in a dealer to show him a treasure your great-grandfather used as a boy back in 1872, and he isn't enthusiastic, remember, you may have one of the uncollectibles. If you're planning an auction on your premises, include these things, and hope for the best. The dealers will see that they bring all they are worth. As my old traveling partner, Frank Rowe, used to say, "Let the bones go with the hide." Such items may add color to a shop, museum, or restoration, but generally make no one any money.

When you buy, remember that old New England farms are full of all sorts of interesting gadgetry. Many are one of a kind, created by the farmer himself to do a specific job. Some approach the Rube Goldberg classification, which may mislead the newcomer into thinking he has uncovered an expensive rarity. Old tools are plentiful but unusable today. They are merely curiosities.

A very fine organization, the Early American Industries Association, Incorporated, has been formed, and publishes a quarterly journal called *The Chronicle*, which delves deeply into the uses of early devices. Such organizations make collectibles of ordinary items, much to the pleasure of dealers and auctioneers, and also help to preserve our history and through their activities acquaint new generations with our former way of life. If you plan to collect early industrial devices, auctions are the best places to frequent. Few dealers like to handle rusty old iron.

My father, who was a businessman, always said, "You make your money when you buy, not when you sell." Think of this before you overpay. While the quickest way to learn is to lose money, there is no need, even for a novice, to get an education this way.

In 1967, in New England, mantel clocks in gingerbread designs hit a new sales high. At auctions, even common ones were bringing thirty-five to forty-five dollars, where a few years before they were selling in the ten- to fifteen-dollar range. The general public, recognizing the increase, quickly flooded the consignment auction barns, hoping to capitalize on clocks that had lain unused for years in barns and attics. The flooding of the market resulted in a quick drop in the value of the clocks, to the extent that in the spring of 1968 one hundred of them, all in working condition, were offered by a dealer at twelve dollars apiece. He found no ready buyers. They are bound to increase in value again, but few people have the money to invest or the space to store such items.

If you buy an item with the possibility of selling it, even within a short time, you need not take a loss. If you go to auctions, seek the advice of the auctioneer. If you patronize good shops, the proprietors are very willing to share their knowledge; they want to satisfy you so you will come back. The idea that there is larceny in the hearts of auctioneers and antique dealers is an unfair generalization. Indeed, dealers themselves are often misled by those who sell them merchandise.

One day, my traveling partner, Frank, who had been buying for over fifty years, added to his education at the age of seventy-three. We had gone to the home of a rather eccentric elderly lady who had called about selling a chest of drawers. It was a bulky Empire piece with elephant-trunk feet. Frank offered her eight dollars, but she held out for ten.

After much dickering, with her reminding Frank what a bargain he was getting, he reluctantly agreed. She no sooner had the ten in hand than she cried out, "At last I beat one of you Rowe boys; we had the house done over, and you can't get that chest out of the room."

She was right. As we tried, she cackled in the kitchen. The old-timer was "taken" by an old lady who had a little larceny in her heart. At last, Frank growled, "Grab the drawers and let's go." Which is what we did, leaving her wailing about what she was going to do with the frame. Frank told her it was a present in return for her kindness. The drawers and the old brasses were sold for five dollars to a cabinetmaker. I asked Frank what lesson he learned that day. He replied, "When you know you're beat, sell out and get out."

Many dealers have learned this lesson, proving that buyer as well as seller must look for every possible hidden detail before any transaction is made. The newcomer to antiques does not have to worry too much. After all, a dealer is a responsible business person who will do all he can to please his customers in order to have them return. All dealers I know will gladly provide a written description of important pieces to serve as a guarantee that the item is what it is represented to be. Merchandise may be returned at a later date if it is determined that the dealer's judgment was not correct and that its value is adversely affected.

One should not be concerned about what profit a dealer or anyone else makes on an item. The basis for buying should be whether the piece is worth what you are willing to pay. Heirs to estates containing valuable antiques should not be expected to give items away just because they have nothing invested in them. Neither should a dealer be expected to sell anything at a greatly reduced price just because he may have made a good buy when he acquired it.

Most competent dealers today do not go into homes and give free appraisals by making offers on antiques. They will ask what the seller's prices are, and say yes or no. The only time offers will be made will be on group purchases, where individual prices are not set. This frustrates those who wish to play dealers against each other. If people resort to tricks to get free appraisals, dealers will protect each other by citing highly inflated values for individual items as they are leaving. Thus the seeker of free information will either never sell the items—no one would pay the price—or else he will sadly part with them for less than dealers' appraisal prices.

But a *proper* appraisal is important; it assures you of getting a fair price for antiques, and the dealer of buying them at a fair price at which he can make a fair profit. New Englanders, who are known to be careful about spending money, are, in the area of antiques, turning more and more to appraisers to assist them when they wish to sell. The small amount paid an appraiser is well worth it. I have never known of a house appraisal where the appraiser didn't earn his fee on one properly appraised item that the owners would have sold for very little. This makes the rest of the appraisal free.

The most competent appraisers come from the ranks of the auctioneers. These men handle everything, from twenty-five-cent trinkets to ten-thousand-dollar antiques. And, being in business year round, they sell these items continuously, which is the best way to keep abreast of prices. Most auctioneers also buy, and by making and losing money on items they never forget their worth. On the other hand, many antique dealers specialize in a narrow range of items and are not aware of values outside their specialized areas. Bank directors, lawyers, insurance and real-estate men, and the nice elderly gentleman down the street make the worst antique appraisers. They are no more qualified to judge the value of used merchandise than an auctioneer would be qualified to run a bank.

Most dealers and auctioneers are happy to see the appraisals done by incompetents, as they can snap up estates containing real "sleepers." The uninitiated can easily mistake a genuine Queen Anne wingback chair for a used Sears, Roebuck, and mark ten dollars on it. Not long ago a Chippendale chair, dug out of a chickencoop, which had not even been included in an inventory because the chickens had roosted on it for years, brought one hundred and fifty dollars at an auction. The auctioneer who bought the estate was also delighted by the many other treasures that turned up. A "nice elderly gentleman down the street" had done the appraisal.

The new buyer must remember that the dealer, whether in New England or elsewhere, also is subjected to the hazards of improper appraisal—either by an owner or in an estate. As Frank Rowe always said, "You have to take the skim milk with the cream." On some items they win; on some they lose; so one must accept the pricing in their shops on this basis. In any case, the law of supply and demand, and competitive pricing, regulate their businesses.

The best place for the newcomer dependent on advice from a dealer to begin buying antiques is at the shops of those who belong to antique-dealer associations, which police their members under a strict code of ethics. If a dealer does not abide by the code, he will not remain a member very long. This does not mean you must be suspicious of dealers who do not belong to such an association, as there are many fine ethical dealers outside associations. I myself have never found a dealer in either category with whom I would not do business again.

The same applies to auctioneers—New England is full of very competent ones. Country auctions and consignment auctions are a way of life, and the local auctioneer is generally respected for his good judgment.

Some time ago a national publication printed an article on fighting auction fever. Why anyone should want to fight it is a mystery to me. The article described it as a malady that slowly creeps into one's system once the auction bug has bitten. After a couple of good purchases, and the subsequent admiration of your friends, you are well on your way toward this "affliction." George A. Martin, a Yankee auctioneer from Maine, always helps things along by admonishing his customers, "Don't think of what you're spending; just think of what you're saving."

Auctions have been a method of selling since the time of the Egyptians. It was accepted as the fairest method of exchange devised by man, and still is today. The majority of estates are liquidated in this manner. Buyers long ago discovered that the best way to acquire items from the past is at auctions, where they can pay what they want. Often, too, items that are unavailable in antique shops keep appearing, and the smart buyer who recognizes values can buy for much less at an auction. Country auctions have become very popular. People can't wait for the good weather so they can get outdoors, take their knitting, and sit and chat with their friends while watching the auction. These are the "sitters and knitters" who don't contribute much to an auction other than local color. Then there are the newly marrieds who eagerly throw their hands up to bid on the fine pieces—and can't understand why the price goes out of reach. The dealers, of course, are also there, sometimes bidding furiously and at other times agreeing not to bid against each other, to keep the prices down, if possible. There are also the old-timers who enjoy giving advice, good or bad. There is the know-it-all who loudly runs down every piece, then bids furiously, hoping he has discouraged others. The outstanding auction-goer is the one who knows where all the merchandise comes from, who owns it, how much was hauled into the house the night before, and who is bidding on his own merchandise. Last and most annoying is the heckler, who delights in attempting to harass the auctioneer with ridiculous bids and who disrupts the proceedings. But generally, auctions are fun, and profitable for both buyer and seller. Under competitive bidding, the seller gets the most for his goods, and under competitive buying you may stop bidding when you wish or go as high as you wish.

Probably the greatest auction of all times took place in England in 1842. Horace Walpole had collected all sorts of early English china from the middle to the latter part of the 1700's. Lord Waldegrave later inherited the china, and disposed of it in an auction that lasted twenty-seven days.

The Auctioneer, a monthly publication issued by the National Auctioneers Association, contains many interesting highlights of the profession. This group is supported by the members of various state auctioneers' associations, pledged to a strict code of ethics prepared by the national group. More and more people are placing their confidence in Association members to run their auctions for them.

At Aalsmeer, a small town near Amsterdam in the Netherlands, the largest flower auction in the world is held. Bidders are faced with a large clock numbered up to one hundred. As a lot comes up, the large hand revolves counterclockwise. The minute the hand reaches a price a buyer is willing to pay, he pushes a button by his seat and the clock stops, signifying he has made the purchase for the dollar figure shown on the clock. In other words, the bidding starts at the top and comes down, rather than going up, as in a regular auction.

Imagine a 330-piece dinnerware set selling at auction for $72,000! The Parke-Bernet Galleries in New York obtained this price for one that had been owned by Josiah Lilly of pharmaceutical fame. It was decorated in eighteen-carat gold, which alone was estimated to be worth about $30,000. The same galleries sold a handwritten document by Abraham Lincoln, on which was a message to the defeated Union Army at the Battle of Fredericksburg, Virginia, for $16,000.

In Mombasa, Kenya, eager buyers snapped up hippo teeth for only

$1.75 a pound at a recent ivory auction sponsored by the Kenya and Uganda governments. Rhinoceros horns brought $10 a pound. Billiard balls, which are made of Calasia ivory, sold at $3 a pound.

In Los Angeles, two Stradivarius instruments, a cello made in 1717 and a viola made in 1728, were put on the block when they were sold by order of the Superior Court. They brought $90,000.

A giant bedstead reputed to have belonged to Shakespeare's mother was purchased for $2,058 at auction in London. The bed was in the estate of a cousin of Winston Churchill.

The auction method of selling is used for just about everything. It is especially helpful in the disposition of estates when there is a clash among the heirs. It establishes prices on one-of-a-kind items for which an intelligent price cannot be set until the items are placed before interested competitive buyers.

With the exception of the Dutch flower auction, auction prices can only go up. With person-to-person dickering, they often go down. Generally, most auction prices are fair to both buyer and seller; if not, there would be no need for auctioneers.

Why not join the club? Here are some tips on how to become an "auction addict" gracefully and successfully.

1. Attend auctions run by members of your state auctioneers' associations or the National Auctioneers Association. These men are pledged to a strict code of ethics that assures you the auctioneer is a businessman with integrity and ability and that he is doing all he can through these associations to upgrade the profession. If you are contemplating having an auction held for you, the same rule applies.

2. Don't hesitate to question the auctioneer as to age, authenticity, and condition of a piece you plan to bid on. It is best to do so before the auction, during inspection time. Responses to such questioning separate the knowledgeable auctioneer from the fly-by-nights, and will result in your being better prepared to bid.

3. Good antiques are a good investment. The best pieces increase in value much more rapidly than any other form of investment. Your auctioneer can guide you to the best pieces.

4. Be content with items you can afford. Don't hesitate to buy items that need repair or refinishing, as they will sell for less money.

5. Beware of friends who are "experts." There are many fine books on antiques. Don't hesitate to question dealers who may be at the auction. They are very helpful to a novice; being so is a good way to cultivate customers.
6. Resist the temptation to sell anything you buy right after you've bought it. Quite often, an opposing bidder will stop bidding to keep the price down, so he can then offer you slightly more than you paid. If this happens, you know you have made a good buy.
7. Don't broadcast how much you paid for something. You may want to sell it someday, and there are some people, especially acquaintances, who are upset at the idea of giving someone a profit. Always buy something with the thought that you may want to sell it—this will prevent you from overbidding.

Fortunately, auctions are held year round. There are many indoor establishments that do consignment selling, and their business is often better in winter than in summer.

Auctions reflect the economy of an area. During a recession, when people need money, the consignment auction business booms as people dispose of unneeded personal possessions. This is a business that increases with hard times. Deaths, divorces, bankruptcies, and depressions in the economy keep the auctioneers very busy.

Sometimes church and charity auctions, where only a few items are involved, supply good pieces at low prices because dealers do not bother to come. Most auctions with donated items have very few of the better pieces, yet if you are there, you can get the good buy. It is also wise to patronize auctions run by new auctioneers. They have not yet built up a following, and while they are getting their education you can generally get good buys. Until a man knows values, he does not know when to sell an item or when to ask more for it.

Auctions can be very exciting in New England, which is why buyers from all over the world go there. At a recent auction in Vermont, there were three cars with foreign license plates. Many English dealers come here to buy English-made antiques out of old estates for shipment back to England, where there now is a shortage of some of their better items. For over a hundred years our dealers shipped them in the other direction.

There seems to be a never-ending supply of old country pieces from New England farmhouses. Yet in recent years similar pieces are becoming available that have the styling of other parts of the country. Of course, antiques from different areas have different characteristics. A piece of Pennsylvania furniture is very unlike its counterpart in New England, and by comparing the workmanship you can easily differentiate between them. One dealer suggested that there are just as many antiques coming into New England from all parts of the country as there are going out. In fact, during the summer it would appear that over 50 percent of New England's antique shops are owned and manned by out-of-staters who buy in their own areas and haul the merchandise to New England to sell during the heart of the tourist season. The kindly shopowner in coveralls who wears an old straw hat and has a wisp of hay between his teeth may be the vice-president of a bank in New Jersey, up here for the summer in a venture he plans to retire to someday. Such people have made a valuable contribution to the economy of many communities in the six states. Many old, deserted farmhouses alongside country roads have been brought back to life and restored to their original gracious appearance, oftentimes with their barns converted to antique shops that attract visitors to the area. The owners buy locally, thus assisting families who have to sell their possessions. They also become customers for many other local businesses.

If you want designs from a particular area, it is best to go directly to that locality for the greatest supply. Thus the best place to buy Sandwich glass is right on the Cape where it was made. Some people feel this is an unlikely area in which to buy, especially during the summer tourist months, but prices are truly reasonable there for good glass.

The public has of course benefited by the increase in antique shows and flea markets that have sprung up all over the countryside. This cooperative effort by dealers provides a central location where buyers can find a huge variety of items and are able to compare prices on the spot. The term "flea market" was borrowed from the open outdoor market that has been held for years in Paris, on the Right Bank, near the Porte de Clignancourt, where insects were almost guaranteed with every sale. Fortunately, the same dividend is not found in this country. Flea markets have become big business, and entrepreneurs compete for the best dealers and locations.

Good country furniture at reasonable prices may be found at roadside flea markets in Vermont, New Hampshire, or Maine. These are not restricted to dealers, and many interesting items turn up. Some people become dealers for a day, rent space to display and dispose of their attic treasures. Get there early in the morning, before the regular dealers have a chance to buy up the better collectibles. Just before closing time is another good time to buy; prices come down on items that dealers are just too tired to move.

The newcomer should not attempt to buy directly out of houses; this is an area hazardous enough for the expert. The beauty of antiques is that so few are identical. On mass-produced items—some china, glassware, and chairs—identical patterns and similarities can be found. But when one buys early furniture, oil paintings, silver, and the like, rarely will two items be exactly alike, unless they were made as a pair, and even then there can be minute differences because of the handwork. Threfore each piece must be submitted to a personal calculated appraisal of what it can be sold for, and on this basis what to pay for it. Such knowledge comes to a dealer only with experience, and you, as a buyer, benefit from experience for which the dealer may have paid dearly in the past. He has earned his profit and has saved you from mistakes. If you are going into the antique business, then plan on making some of the mistakes that come from buying out of homes. It is a quick but costly way to learn.

Some communities do not permit auctions within their boundaries (these laws should be challenged by auctioneers; many consider them unconstitutional). These rulings will be found in the three southern states, but not in the three northern ones. As a result, there are people who specialize in what is known as a house sale. They will do this for executors or will buy the estate and handle the sale themselves. Prices are set on all items, and a salesperson is placed in each room. These seem to be extremely successful, and for good reason. Crowds line up early, and within a few hours the walls are bare. The executors may not know that the pricing has been done so badly that knowledgeable people are walking out with tremendous bargains. At two house sales I attended, I was shocked at the ridiculous pricing of some items, and wondered how the executors would feel if they knew how they had unknowingly deprived their clients of a fairer return that would have rightly come to them through competitive auction bidding. In one home, a pair of rare jadeite figurines from the Orient were whipped out for two hundred dollars before I could get my hands on them. They were worth nearer two thousand. Go to such house sales for the buys of a lifetime. This is the one area of real giveaways in antiques today. The sooner executors realize this, and encourage the placement of goods in the hands of a capable auctioneer in a more friendly area, the sooner will clients get true value for their pieces.

It is amazing that so many fine antiques still find their way to the open market. With today's awareness of the value of antiques, most people give or leave them to members of their families to be handed down to future generations. Yet, when a piece does leave the family circle, it is interesting to know through how many hands it can pass. At a recent antique show in Massachusetts, a dealer purchased a pair of Mary Gregory decorated vases from another dealer. This dealer now owned them for the second time, as she had originally purchased them from an elderly lady in her hometown; she had then sold them to a collector, who later sold them to the dealer she bought them from at the show. Along came a young couple looking for some Mary Gregory glass. An alert dealer went to the booth that originally had them and then tracked them to the new dealer-owner. He purchased them on the spot, giving that dealer a profit, and returned to his booth to resell them within minutes. The young couple was delighted with the pair; it reminded them of a similar pair owned by the girl's grandmother. The end of the story is obvious. When the dealers compared notes, they realized that the original seller was the girl's grandmother—the vases had passed through four sets of hands within a couple of weeks to get to the granddaughter. Everyone made a profit along the way.

A few years ago, some New Hampshire people, traveling in England, paid a huge sum for an old oak carved chair that had inscribed on its back the fact that it was made from a pew that came from a church in which William Shakespeare had worshiped. At the settling of the estate many years later, the chair was sold at auction for $35. It was an interesting simple side chair, but not one that aroused dealers to speculate on it. The buyer attempted to sell it at a profit for over a year, and then, in desperation, while manning his booth at a show in Rhode Island, sold it to another dealer for $25. This dealer tried to sell it at a profit, but with no luck. Finally, at an auction late in the season, it was sold for $22.50 to new owners who seemed to be buying it because they liked Shakespeare and not because they thought the chair had antique value. As this example shows, there is no formula for judging desirability. The item had everything "going" for it, yet it resulted only in lost money.

It had rarity—perhaps another will never be seen in this country. It had age—the wood was wormeaten and scarred; it was put together by joining and pegs. It had documentation, inscribed on its back. It related to a very famous person who might very well have sat on it at one time. It was on sale at reasonable prices for well over a year. Surely, in all that time, many people should have expressed an interest in it, even if only as a curiosity. Yet it lay unsold. Thus desirability sets value —not rarity; not documentation; not handmade construction; not period or any other quality or attribute. No matter how fine or interesting a piece is, if no one wants it, it has no value.

The year 1976 is going to be our bicentennial, and every facet of our colonial life is going to be explored and exploited. New interest will be aroused in our antiquities, and greater demand will result in greater prices. Anyone interested in collecting early American should begin now. Many fine pieces rise in value so quickly that one could borrow money at 7 percent today to buy them and still come out ahead in the future. The best pieces increase in value even faster, and today represent an excellent investment. Prices are rising to the extent that it is becoming more and more difficult to acquire what you want without a great deal of money.

Though many antiques are now selling for less than reproductions, this will not always be true. Old country pine and maple pieces will soon overtake the new ones in price. Even such a fine piece as a Sheraton sofa is now approximately the same price as a new one. This is bound to change by the time of the bicentennial.

The best investments at this time are oil paintings and furniture of the proper period and by the best craftsmen. These will always command top prices, and they will continue to rise in scarcity and value. The next best investment is early American silver. Its increase in value is astounding everyone.

If you have limited funds, there are still many interesting areas in which to speculate. Bottles, both old and new, are very good, yet relatively inexpensive. Lithographed souvenir china, which was made at the beginning of this century, with its scenes of town halls, fairgrounds, main streets, and so on, is bound to come into its own as a historically interesting, colorful, yet still inexpensive collectible. Much "carnival" glasses is still available, and because it represents an interesting period in glassmaking, it is important.

Historical books, which already have climbed in price, will continue to rise in value. At the time of our bicentennial, much historical writing and research will be done. And since most libraries do not have space or facilities to house other than relatively known works, writers who want new material will look for the little-known history books, diaries, or personal accounts of particular sections of the country.

Because many amateur and professional drama groups will put on plays and pageants reflecting our early life, there will be a need for period clothing. Such articles may not increase greatly in value, but some money can be made if they are bought now and held until the bicentennial.

Old wagons, carriages, sleighs, and automobiles will be in demand for parades or display. But a word of warning concerning old cars: purchasing them from the general public is difficult. Because knowledgeable buyers resist inflated prices, many antique cars are rusting away in barns and garages, and, consequently, deteriorating in value. If you own one, it may be unwise to hold on to it. Condition is very important to its eventual sales price. It may be depreciating faster than the demand for it will increase. It is much easier and cheaper to buy from among the hundreds of restored cars continually advertised in club and association journals devoted to this type of collecting. If you want an old car, locate the nearest antique-car club. From its members and through its literature you will learn of hundreds of old cars for sale at prices that are still reasonable. Get your "antique" car now to avoid the inflated prices of 1976.

Index

Index

Aalsmeer (Netherlands) flower auction, 177, 178
Aborn, James, 54
Acanthus-leaf design, 36
Adam, James, 28
Adam, Robert, 28
Adams, Lemuel, 54
Agata glassware, 69
Alden, John, 14
Allis, John, 14
Amberg, Louis, 138
Amberina glass, 68, 79, 160
American Carnival Glass Association, 75
American Home Period, 46
American Pottery Co., 83
Andirons, 113
Andrew, John, 131
Andrews, Isaac, 131
Animal designs
  iron banks, 142, 143
  pottery, 5, 81, 83–84, 87–88
Anne, Queen, 21
  See also Queen Anne Period
Antique Trader, 77
Antiques
  appraisals, 174–175, 181

auctions and auctioneers, 175, 176–179, 181
books on, 162, 171, 179
"camp," 4–6
collecting, 162, 170–184
  See also specific items, periods, etc.
dealers, 174, 175–176
definition of, 171
desirability and value of, 182–183
farmhouse, 179–181
flea markets, 180
house sales, 181–183
as investments, 7, 178, 183–184
sources, 170, 171, 172–183
tips on buying and selling, 170–184
value (prices), 1, 4, 6, 170–184
  See also specific craftsmen, items, periods, etc.
Apothecary Shop, Shelburne Museum, Vt., 77
Appleton, Nathaniel, 54
Appliquéd bed coverings, 165–166
Appraisals, 174–175, 181
Arcade Manufacturing Co., 141

Ardabil rugs, 164
Armor, 169
Arnold, Thomas, 131
Arrowheads, 1
Art (artists)
    contemporary, 151, 155
    etchings, 153
    exhibitions, 151, 152
    folk, 165
    line engravings, 153
    lithographs, 153–154
    oils, 146–152
        See also Oil paintings
    pottery, 96–97
    prints, 153–155
    reproductions, 153–155
    woodcuts, 153
    See also specific artists, crafts,
        locations, etc.
Art glass, ix, 68
    See also Glass; specific items
Art Nouveau Period, 4–6
Ash wood, use of, 2
Attics, ix
Auctioneer, The, 177
Auctioneers, 175, 176–179, 181
Auctions, 171, 172, 173, 175, 176–
        179, 181
    bidding, 176–177, 178
    church and charity, 179
    consignment, 179
    country, ix, 176–177
    tips on, 178–179
Augie Doggie, 145
Austin, Ebeneezer, 131
Austin, James, 131
Austin, Nathaniel, 123, 131
Austin, Richard, 123
Autographs, 161, 177
Automobiles, 184

Badger, James, 147
Badger, Thomas, 123
Badlam, Stephen, Jr., 54
Bagnall, Benjamin, 101
Bagnall, Samuel, 101
Bailey, Charles A., 141–142
Bailey, T., 151
Ball, John, 131
Ball-and-claw foot, 26
Baltimore, Md., 2
Bamboo furniture, 46
Bangkok, ceramics from, 94
Banjo clocks, 104, 105, 106
Banks, 141–144
    designs, 141–143
    iron, 113, 141–144
    mechanical, 143
    prices (values), 142, 143
    tin, 141, 142
Banquet tables, 32
Barbie dolls, 145
Barns, antiques in, ix, 1
    See also Farmhouses
Barret, Richard Carter, 83–84
Bartlett, Nathaniel, 131
Barton, Charles, 123
Bath, Me., Marine Museum, 151
Beakers, pewter, 121
Beck, Isaac, 131
Bed coverings, 164–167
Bedroom suites, 7
Beds
    bamboo, 46
    brass, 4, 119
    coverings, 164–167
    folding, 28
    four-poster, 7
    hide-a-way, 4
    iron, 4
    tall pine, 42
    Victorian, 39, 42

Bedwarmers, 116
Beech wood, use of, 2
    See also specific items
Belcher, David, 123
Belcher, Joseph, 123
Belding, Samuel, 14
Belleek ware, 82, 97–98
Bells, iron, 114
Belter, John Henry, 37
Benches, 14
Benefit Street restoration, Providence, R.I., 8
Benjamin, John, 131
Benjamin, Samuel, 54
Bennington (Vt.) ware, 83, 84–87
Bentley, Thomas, 131
Bentwood chairs, 49
Betty lamps, 114, 157
Bewick, Thomas, 153
Bible boxes, 16
Bibles, 16, 161
Bicentennial, U.S., 183–184
    furniture, 45–46
Bierstadt, Albert, 147, 149
Bijar rugs, 164
Billings, William, 123
Birch wood, use of, 2, 10, 21, 34, 39, 49
    See also specific items
Bird's-eye maple wood, 34
Bisc Novelty Co., 138
Bisque, 98
    dolls, 138, 140
Blackburn, Joseph, 147
Blacksmiths, 112, 113
    See also Iron
Blaisdell, David, 102
Blake, Judson, 54
Blanket chests, 40
    pine lift-top, 40, 145
Blankets, wool, 167

Bleachers, iron, 112
Blockfront chests, 45, 53
Blowers, John, 131
Blue Cornflower glass, 68
Boardman, Thomas, 123
Bog iron, 111, 112
Bohemian-style restorations, 8
Bonin pottery, 83
Books
    on antiques, reading, 162, 171, 179
    historical, collecting, 161–162, 184
Booth, Ebeneezer, 54
Booth, Elijah, 54
Booth, Joel, 54
Boston, Mass.
    cabinetmakers, 21, 39, 45
    copper and brass manufacture, 118
    glass, 56, 61
    Museum of Fine Arts, 125
    oil portraitists, 147
    pewterers, 123
    pottery, 87, 89
    Queen Anne Period, 21
    restorations, 8
    Scollay Square, 8
    silverwork, 130, 131
    town houses, 6, 8
    Victorian Period, 39, 45
Boston and Sandwich Glass Works, 56–61, 89
Boston Crown Glass Co., 56
Boston Porcelain and Glass Co., 56
Bottles, 5, 55, 56, 63, 71, 75–79
    bitters, 75
    colors, 75, 76
    commemorative, 78, 79
    documenting, 71, 76

Bottles (*cont.*)
  figurals, 75
  flasks, 63, 75–79
  historicals, 75, 76
  identification, 71
  investing in, 76, 77, 79, 183
  liquor, 77–79
  medicinals, 75, 77
  new, 77–79
  pontil marks, 71
  values (prices), 76–77, 78–79, 183
Boudoir clocks, 104
Bourbon bottles, 77–78
Bowls, glass, 56
Braided rugs, 163
Braintree, Mass., 111, 112
Brass, 116–119
  decorations, 4, 45
  documentation, 117
  plated, 116–117
  prices (values), 113, 116–117
  See also specific items
Bread platters, railroad-train, 76
Brewster, Abel, 131
Bridge, John, 131
Brigdon, Zachariah, 131
Bristol glazed pottery, 89, 95
Britannica (metal), 120, 122
British, see England (English)
Brittany stoneware, 98
Broilers, iron, 114
Bronzes, 4, 5, 118–119
  cloisonné, 119
  enameling, 119
  gilded (ormolu), 118
  prices (values), 118
  See also specific items
Brown, Gawen, 102
Brown, John, Providence, R.I., house of, 53

Bru doll, 140
Buell, Abel, 131
Buffalo, N.Y., Elmwood Avenue restoration, 8
Bull's-eye glass panes, 71
Burgham, John, 149
Burnham, Benjamin, 54
Burr, Ezekiel, 131
Burr, Nathaniel, 131
Burrill, Samuel, 131
Burt, John, 131
Burt, Samuel, 131
Burt, William, 131
Butler, James, 131
Buttons, 116, 168

Cabinet Maker's London Book of Prices and Designs (Shearer), 28
Cabinetmaking, development of, 2, 9 ff., 28, 35–36 ff., 54
  See also Carvings (carvers); Furniture and furnishings; specific cabinetmakers, items
Cabinets, 28
  See also Chests of drawers
Cabriole legs, 21, 23, 26
Calder, William, 123
Calendar clocks, 106
"Camp" antiques, 4–6
Canada
  china and pottery, 97–98
  furniture, 14, 39
Candelabra, 104, 121
Candia, N.H., 54
Candleholders (candlesticks), 104, 112, 114, 115, 116, 121, 156–159
  age, 156
  brass, 116

glass, 63
pewter, 121
Candles, 156–159
Candlesticks, see Candleholders (candlesticks)
Cane chairs, 40, 49
Canning jars, glass, 76
Cans, tin, 115
Canteens, 169
Cantonware, 95
Capo di Monte ware, 98
Cardboard fans, 167
Carder glass, 73
Caribbean area, 10, 19
Carlile, John, 54
Carnival glass, 73–75, 170, 184
Carriages, antique, 184
    doll, 138
Cars, antique, 184
Carvings (carvers), 9–54
    value determination, 43
    See also Cabinetmaking, development of; Furniture and furnishings; specific individuals, items, periods, etc.
Casey, Gideon, 131
Catherine of Braganza, 50
Celadon porcelain, 95
Celluloid dolls, 135
Centennial furniture, 45
Ceramics, see Pottery
Chains, iron, 112–113
Chairs
    Art Nouveau, 4
    bentwood, 49
    cane, 40, 49
    Carver-type, 2
    Chippendale, 26, 28
    Hepplewhite, 29
    Hitchcock, 41
    Morris, 4, 6

paintings on, 149
pine, 40–42
potty, 7
Queen Anne, 21, 23
rockers, 6, 41, 46
Shaker ladderback, 48–49
stretchers, 16, 23
Victorian, 39, 40–42, 44
William and Mary, 16, 20
Windsor, 41–42
Chamber pots, 5, 87
Chamber sets, 5, 87
Chambers, Thomas, 149
Champney, Benjamin, 147
Chapin, Eliphalet, 54
Chargers, pewter, 121
Charles II, 50
Charlestown, Mass., cabinetmakers, 54
Charlotte (doll), 140
Chasing silver process, 128
Chelmsford, Mass., glass, 56
Chelsea, Mass.
    Keramic Art Works, 87
    potteries, 87
        "Chelsea Faience" marking, 87
Cherry wood, use of, 10, 21, 34, 47
Chest-on-chest, 21–23
Chest-on-frame, 15, 21–23
Chestnut wood, use of, 2
    See also specific items
Chests
    Art Nouveau ("camp"), 4
    blanket, 40
    blockfront, 45
    Centennial, 45
    Chippendale, 23, 26
    dollhouse, 144–145
    on frames, 14, 21–23
    Frothingham, 53

Chests (*cont.*)
  Hadley, 14–15
  marriage, 16
  Pilgrim, 14–16
  present-day, 47–48
  Queen Anne, 21, 23–26
  Sheraton, 32
  storage, 40
  tall, 15, 16, 21, 145
  Victorian, 39–40
  William and Mary, 16, 19, 21
Chicago, Ill., Olde Town restoration, 8
Children's artifacts
  banks, 141–144
  clothing, 144
  dollhouses and furniture, 144–145
  dolls, 134–141
  games, 144, 145
  toys, 138, 143–146
Chime clocks, 104, 106
Ch'in (Huai) Period bronzes, 118
China
  -cased clocks, 104, 109
  export porcelain, 94–95
  -headed dolls, 138
  imports, 3–4, 94–95
  porcelain, 82, 84–87, 89, 94–95
  souvenir, lithographed, 183–184
China (country)
  bronzes, 118
  ceramics, 3–4, 80, 81, 94–95, 104, 109, 138
  export porcelain, 94–95
  furniture, influence of, 26
  rugs from, 164
Chippendale, Thomas, 10, 23, 26–29
Chippendale Period, 10, 13, 23, 26–29

Chou-culture bronzes, 118
Chronicle, The, 173
Church and charity auctions, 179
Church pewter, 121
Churchill, Winston S., 1, 178
Circular saw, 48
Circus figure toys, 143
City furniture, 11, 34
  See also specific items, periods, places, etc.
Civil War
  dolls, 139
  firearms, 168
  iron banks, 141
  Lincoln autograph, 177
  swords, 169
  wooden canteens, 169
CKAW (pottery marking), 87
Claggett, Thomas, 102
Claggett, William, 102
Clark, Jonathan, 131
Classic style, 36–37
Clay, use of, 2, 80 ff., 89
  See also Pottery; specific items
Clay dolls, 134
Clement, Arthur W., 162
Clocks, 99–110
  bronze, 5
  buying, 109–110
  can weights, 103
  cases, 103, 104–106, 110
  Chippendale, 26
  clockmakers, 99–106
  designs, 104, 105, 106
  electric, 105
  gadgetry, 104
  handwork, 102–103
  identification, 103, 105–106
  mantel, 100, 104, 106–109, 173
  pendulum, 99, 105

prices (values), 102–103, 105–110
repairing, 109
shelf, 100, 104
spring-driven, 100, 104
tall (grandfather), 100, 101, 102, 103, 104
wall, 105
weights, 99–101, 103, 104
wooden works, 100–101
woods, 103
Cloisonné, 119
Cloth dolls, 134, 141
Clothespins, 48
Clothing
  children's, 144
  doll, 134, 139–140
  period, 173, 184
Coblenz, Germany, decorated stoneware, 80
Coburn, John, 131
Coffee pots, 116, 128
Coffee roasters, iron, 114
Coffee sets, silver, 127–128
Coffee tables, 5
Coin silver, 131
Cole, Thomas, 147
Cole, Timothy, 153
Collecting (collectors), 1–8, 170–184
  See also Antiques; specific items, periods, sources, etc.
Cologne, Germany, decorated stoneware, 80
Colt (Samuel) firearms, 168
Comic-strip banks, 142
Commemorative
  booklets, 162
  bottles, 78, 79
Commodes, lift-top, 39–40
Concord, Mass., cabinetmaking, 54

Concord, N.H., Historical Society, 54
Coney, John, 130
Connecticut
  cabinetmakers, 54
  clocks, 99, 101, 103, 104
  metal pieces, 112, 115, 122–123
  pewterers, 122–123
  See also specific items, towns, cities, craftsmen, individuals
Consignment auctions, 4, 179
Cookie jars, 5
Cooking utensils, 114–115, 116
  See also specific items
Copley, John Singleton, 147
Copper, 116–118
  documentation, 117
  engravings, 153
  and pewter, 119
  plated, 116–117
  prices (values), 113, 116–117
"Cottage furniture," 39
Country fairs, 151
Country furniture, 11, 34–39, 44, 49, 180–181
  See also specific items, periods, places
Court cupboards, 16
Cousins, Frank, 162
Coventry, Vt., cabinetmakers, 54
Coventry flask, 76
Coventry Glass Works, 63
Coverlets, figured, 165
Cowell, William, Sr. and Jr., 131
Crackleware, 87
Craftsmanship, 2–3 ff.
  See also Cabinetmaking; Carvings; specific craftsmen, materials, periods, places, etc.
Cranberry glass, 64, 68

Crawford House, Boston, Mass., 8
Creamers, silver, 128
Crewelwork, 167
Crocks, stoneware, 5, 81, 89
Cropsey, Jasper, 147
Cross, Peter, 83
Crusie lamps, 114, 157
Crystal Lake, N.H., bog iron, 112
Cupboards, 16, 53
Currier, Nathaniel, and Ives, J. M., 154
Curtis, Bette, 141
Curtis, Lemuel, 106
Cuspidors, pewter, 121
Cut glass, 72

Daguerreotypes, 162
Danforth, Edmond, 122
Danforth, John, 122
Danforth, Joseph, 122
Danforth, Josiah, 122
Danforth, Thomas, 122
Danforth family, 122–123
Danish modern furniture, 47
Davis, W. O., 64
Dealers, ix–x, 1, 43–44, 174, 175–176, 181
Dedham (Mass.) Pottery, 87–88
Deeds, 161
Delftware, 98
Dennis, Thomas, 54
Derby, Thomas, 123
Designs and designers, 10 ff.
  Adam brothers, 28
  Art Nouveau, 4, 5
  foreign influences, 10–11 ff.
    See also specific countries, items, periods
  iron banks, 141–144
  Pilgrim (Jacobean), 16
  Queen Anne, 21–26

William and Mary, 16
  See also specific designers, designs, items, periods, places, etc.
Desks
  Frothingham, 53
  Queen Anne, 23–24
  secretary, 23–24
  slant-top, 2, 23
  Tiffany sets, 73
Dining-room sets, 7
  See also specific items, periods
Dinnerware, 87, 177
  See also specific items
Disbrowe, Nicholas, 14
Dishes
  china, 96–98
  pewter, 121
Documentation, 3, 14 ff., 21, 45
  See also specific items, periods
Documents, historical, 161
Dollar pocket watches, 104–105, 110
Dollhouses, 138, 144–145
Dolls, 134–141
  age, 135, 139
  carriages, 138
  closed-mouth, 139
  clothing, 134, 139–140
  dollmakers, 137–141
  foot and shoe style, 139
  hair, 139
  handmade, 140–141
  houses, 138, 144–145
  identification, 139
  imports, 134, 135, 136, 138–139, 140–141
  values (prices), 139
Dorchester, Mass., cabinetmakers, 54
Dorchester (Mass.) Pottery, 89–94

Doughnut kettles, 114
Doughty, Thomas, 147
Drawers
    Centennial, 45
    checking for period authenticity, 20, 23, 45
    Empire Period, 37
    overhanging top, 37
    pulls, 37
Dreppard, Carl, 162
Dropleaf tables, 40
Duckfoot legs, 21
Dunham, Rufus, 115, 123
Dunlap, John, 53, 54
Dunlap, Samuel, II, 53, 54
Dunlap Circle, 11–13, 26, 53–54
Durand, Asher, 147
Durand glass, 73
Dutch
    flower auction, 177, 178
    furniture, 15, 26
    imports, 23
    pottery, 81, 98
    silver, 126

Early American Industries Association, 173
Earthenware, 80–98
East Windsor, Conn., 54
Eclipse Manufacturing Co., 138
Edison, Thomas A., 138
Egan, Matthew, 54
Egyptians, 15
Eisenhower, Dwight D., 79
Electric clocks, 105
Electric train sets, 144
Elephant-trunk foot design, 36
Elfreth's Alley, Philadelphia, Pa., 8
Elgin watches, 104
Ellis, Joel, 137–138

Elm wood, use of, 2, 10, 20
    See also specific items
Elmwood Avenue area restoration, Buffalo, N.Y., 8
Embroidered rugs, 163
Empire Period, 13, 35–37
England (English)
    brass, 116
    clocks, 99, 104
    earthenware and porcelain, 80–81, 82, 83, 84–87, 88, 94–97
    exports to, 179
    furniture and furnishings, 2–3, 10, 11, 13, 19–20, 21–23, 34, 50–52
    identification, 19–20
    imports from, 19–20, 39
    pewter, 119–120
    silver, 125, 127
    tinware, 115
    See also specific individuals, items, periods, places, etc.
Engravings
    line, 153
    silver, 128
Estates, 175, 178, 181–182
Etchings, 153
Etruscan majolica, 88–89
Europe, see Imports; specific countries, individuals, items, periods
Exhibitions, painting, 152

Fairbairn, Mrs. Mary, 87–88
Fairs, country, 151
Faneuil Hall, Boston, Mass., 8
Fans, 167–168
    cardboard, 167
    carvings, 26
    ivory, 167–168

Fans (*cont.*)
  mirror, 167
  silk, 167, 168
Farmhouses as source of antiques,
      ix, 1, 49, 172–173, 179–180
  See also Barns
Father, Gwen, 141
"Favrile" (Tiffany mark), 73
Federal Period, 13, 33–34
  houses, 6, 7
  See also Hepplewhite Period;
      Sheraton Period
Feke, Robert, 147
Fenton, Christopher Webber, 83
Fenton Pottery, 82, 83
Figure-light clocks, 105, 106
Firearms, 168–169
Firepans, iron, 114
Fireplaces, 7
  equipment, 113, 114, 115, 116
  See also specific items
First National Bank, Chicago, Ill.,
      commemorative bottles, 78
Fisher, Alvin, 147
Fitzhugh porcelain, 95
Flasks, 63
  eagle design, 63
  historical, 75
  Masonic, 63, 76
  Sunburst, 63, 76
Flatiron Building iron bank, 143
Flea markets, 1, 145, 151, 180–181
Floor coverings, 163
Floral designs, use of, 5, 42
  See also specific items
Flying-saucer banks, 143
Folding beds, 78
Foreign imports and influence, *see*
      Imports; specific countries,
      individuals, items, periods
Foster, John, 153

Foster, Joseph, 63
Frames, picture, 5, 150
France (French), 3
  china, 98
  clocks, 104
  dolls, 134, 136, 138, 140
  fans, 168
  furniture and furnishings, 10, 21,
      26, 36, 52
    See also specific items, indi-
        viduals, periods
Fredericksburg (Va.), Battle of,
      177
Fritzi Ritz (paper doll), 136
Frost, Robert, doll, 141
Frothingham, Benjamin, 11, 53,
      54
Frothinghams (cabinetmakers of
      Boston, Mass.), 11, 53, 54
Fruit-design
  banks, 141
  furniture carvings, 43
  glass, 75
Frying pans, iron, 115
Fulper Potteries, 138
Furniture and furnishings, 9–54
  Bicentennial, 45–46, 183–184
  "camp" (Art Nouveau), 4–6
  city, 11, 34
  country, 11, 34–39, 44, 49, 180–
      181
  documentation, 3, 14 ff., 21, 45
    See also specific items, manu-
        facturers, periods
  dollhouse, 144–145
  foreign influences, *see* Imports;
      specific countries, items, pe-
      riods, places
  investing in, 183
  transitional period, 24

veneers and inlays, see Veneers and inlays

See also Cabinetmaking; specific craftsmen, individuals, items, manufacturers, periods, places, woods

Gadroon silver border design, 128–130

Gaines, John, III, 54

Game tables, 29, 34

Games, children's, 144, 145

Gateleg tables, 19

Gebrüder Heubach dolls, 140

Germany
  clocks, 104
  dolls, 134, 135, 136, 137, 138, 140
  pottery, 80, 81, 89, 98

Gillam, Charles, 54

Gilmanton (N.H.) Iron Works, 112

Glass, 55–79
  art-, ix, 68
  attribution, 63, 69, 71, 79
  bottles, 55, 56, 63, 71, 75–79
    See also Bottles
  bowls, 56
  Carnival, 73–75, 170, 184
  colors, 56, 63, 68, 75, 79
  cut, 72
  designs, 63–69
  documenting, 3, 55, 69, 71
  flasks, 63, 75
  glass makers, 55 ff., 71, 76
  Imperial, 75
  insulators, 76
  iridescent, 4, 72–75
  lamps, 160
  marks, 63, 71, 75
  molds, 71
  pressed, 56, 64
  ringing sound test, 72
  Tiffany, 4, 72–73, 170
  values, 73, 79
  vases, 56
  window, 2, 55, 63, 71

Glassblowers, 3, 55 ff., 71, 76

Glazing, 80–81, 83, 87, 89

Gleason, Roswell, 123

Glue, in chests, 15

Goddards (cabinetmakers of Rhode Island), 11, 53, 54

Gold watches, 110

Goldsmith (Philip) Company, 138

Gone with the Wind lamp, 160

Grandfather clocks, 100, 101, 102, 103, 104, 105

Grandmother clocks, 105

Granite Glass Co., 63

Graniteware, 83, 87

Grape design
  furniture, 43
  pottery, 84

Great Britain, see England (English)

Great Chain, 112

Greatback, Daniel, 83–84

Greek motifs, 50

Green, Samuel, 123

Greenaway, Kate, 144

Greene, Rufus, 131

Gregory (Mary) vases, 182

Greiner, Ludwig, 137

Griswold, Ashbil, 123

Guilds, silversmiths, 127

Gunderson glass, 73

Guns, 168–169

Gunstock Mountain, iron from, 112

Gutenberg, Johannes, 153

Hadley chests, 14–15

Hamadan rugs, 164

Hamilton watches, 104

Hamlin, Samuel, 123

Hammerslough, Philip, 162

Hammersmith iron, 111

Hampshire Pottery, 88–89

Handcraftsmanship, 2–3, 36
  value of, 50
  See also specific craftsmen, items, periods, etc.

Hanover Hotel, Boston, Mass., 8

Hardin, William, 131

Hardwoods, 2, 42
  See also specific items, woods

Harold's Club, Reno, Nev., souvenir bottles, 78

Hartford, Conn., cabinetmakers, 54

Hatfield, Conn., 14

Hatfield, Mass., 14

Haviland, David, 98

Henderson, George, 89

Hennessey, William, 149

Hepplewhite, George, 10, 28, 29–32, 34–35

Hepplewhite Period, 7, 13, 20, 28, 29–32, 34–35, 53
  See also Federal Period

Hewes, Robert, 55–56

Hickory wood, 49

Hide-a-beds, 4

Highboys, 16, 21, 145
  See also Chests

Hill, Charles A., 89

Hill, John, 149

Hill, Thomas, 149

Hinckley, Henrietta, 138

Historical artwork, 151, 155

"Historical Blues" (English chinaware), 96–97

Historical books, 161, 184

Historical figures, dolls of, 140–141

Hitchcock chairs, 41

HO toy train sets, 144

Hoadley, Silas, 103

Hobbs and Brocunier Co., 72

Home-improvement items, 46
  See also specific items

Homes, William, 131

Hong Kong, ceramics from, 94

Hook, William, 54

Hooked rugs, 163

Horse-drawn toy fire engines, 143

Horsehair coverings, 29, 44

Hosmer, Joseph, 54

Hotchkiss, Arthur, 138

Hound-handle pitchers, 84

House sales, 181–183

Household artifacts, 3, 46
  See also specific items, periods

Houses
  Federal style, 6
  period, interest in, 6–7
  town, 6–8
  Victorian, 6

How to Identify Bennington Pottery, 83–84

Howard, Edward, 105

Howard, Thomas, Jr., 54

Howe, Elias, 172

Hudson River School artists, 147

Hunneman brass and copper, 116, 117

Hurd, Isaac, 131

Hurd, Jacob, 131

Hurd, Nathaniel, 131

Hussey Manufacturing Co., 112

Identification, 9, 49
  English and American pieces, 19–20
  by period, 13 ff.
  See also specific craftsmen, items, manufacturers, places, etc.
Imperial glass, 73–75
Imperial Glass Works, 73–75
Imports, 3–4
  clocks, 99, 103, 104
  dolls, 134, 135, 136, 138–139, 140–141
  earthenware and porcelain, 3–4, 82, 83, 84, 94–98
  furniture and furnishings, 3–4, 9, 39, 50–52
  glass, 79
  metal artifacts, 114, 115, 116
  See also specific countries, items, periods
Indians, American
  arrowheads, 1
  dolls, 134
  medicine bottles, 77
  pottery, 1, 82–83
  tomahawk heads, 1
Industrial devices, 173
Ingersoll watches, 104–105, 110
Inkwells, glass, 63
Inlays, *see* Veneers and inlays
Inness, George, 147
Insulators, glass, 76
Investments, antique purchases as, 7, 178, 183–184
Ipswich, Mass., cabinetmakers, 54
Iran, rugs from, 164
Ireland, Belleek stoneware from, 82, 97–98

Iridescent glass, 4, 72–75
Iron, 3, 111–115
  banks, 113, 141–144
  beds, 4
  bog iron, 112
  candleholders, 114, 157
  cooking utensils, 114–115
  documenting, 111, 113
  fireplace, 113, 114
  kettles, 113, 114
  lamps, 5, 113, 114, 157
  locks, 15
  prices (values), 111, 113
  sources of, 111–112
  toys, 143
Ironstone, 84–87
Italy
  furniture, 47, 52
  pottery, 81, 98
Ives, J. M., 154
Ivory fans, 167–168

Jacobean (Pilgrim) Period, 13–16
Jacques, William, 138
Japan
  ceramics, 89
  dolls, 140
  rugs, 164
Jarves, Deming, 56–61
Jerome, Chauncey, 101
Jersey City, N.J., pottery, 83, 84
Jim Beam Distilling Co., commemorative bottles, 77–78
Johnson, Thomas, 102
Jones, Gershom, 123
Jugs
  silver, 128
  stoneware, 5, 81, 89, 90
Jumeau doll, 140

Keene, N.H.
   glass, 63, 76
   pottery, 88–89
Kellegi (Oriental rug size), 164
Kenareh (Oriental rug size), 164
Kennedy, John F., 79
Kensett, John, 147
Kenton Hardware Company iron
      banks, 141
Kerosene oil lamps, 159
Kettles, iron, 113–114
Key-wind watches, 109–110
King, Wallace, 88
Kingston, N.Y., pottery remnants,
      82
Kitchen
   chairs, 4, 7, 40–42
   earthenware, 82
   ranges, 7
   tables, 4, 7
   utensils, 4, 46, 113, 114–115, 116
   See also specific items, kinds of
      material, periods, etc.

Ladder back chairs, 48–49
Lake Dunmore Glass Co., 64
Lalique glass, 73
Lamps, 4, 5, 156–160
   collecting, 156–160
   mahogany, 5
   metal, 112, 114, 116, 121
   whale-oil, 113, 159
Lampstands, 40
Landscape paintings, 146, 147–
      150, 151
Lane, John, 54
Lanterns, 115, 116
Leather dolls, 135
Ledgers, store, 161
Lee, Richard, 122
Lee, Richard, Jr., 122

Legs, furniture
   Adam brothers, 28
   cabriole, 21, 23, 26
   fluted design, 28
   Hepplewhite, 28, 32
   Pilgrim, 14, 15
   Queen Anne, 21, 23, 26
   Shearer, 28
   Sheraton, 35
   square tapered, 28
   tapered, 28, 32
   William and Mary, 16, 19
Leighton, Thomas, 72
Lift-top commodes, 39–40
Lighting devices, 156–160
   See also specific kinds
Lilly, Josiah, 177
Lily-pad glass design, 63
Limoges porcelain, 98
Lincoln, Abraham
   autographs, 177
   era (American Home Period),
      46
Lind, Jenny, paper doll, 137
Linsey-woolseys, 165
"Lion passant" touchmark, 127
Liquor bottles, 77–79
Lithographed souvenir china, 183
Lithographs, 153–155
Little Women dolls, 140
Locks
   Bible box, 16
   iron, 15
Looms, 171–172
Loring, Joseph, 131
Lowestoft china, 94–95
Lynde, Thomas, 131
Lyre design, Empire Period, 36

Machine power tools, use of, 3,
      35–36, 39, 52, 53

McIntire, Samuel, 24, 54, 162
McKinley Tariff Law, 3
Magazines, antique, 162
Mahogany furniture and furnish-
    ings, 5, 7, 10, 11, 53
  crotched, 16
  Queen Anne Period, 21
  Sheraton Period, 34
  Victorian Period, 42
  William and Mary Period, 16, 19
Maiden's-blush cranberry glass, 64
Maine
  cabinetmakers (before 1830), 54
  pewterers, 122, 123
  See also specific craftsmen, loca-
    tions, manufacturing com-
    panies, and products
Majolica, 88–89
Maker, Jeannie, 141
Mantel clocks, 100, 104, 106–109
  Chippendale, 28
  gingerbread design, 173
  prices (values), 173
Manufacturing techniques, intro-
    duction of, 3
  See also Machine power tools,
    use of
Maple-wood furniture, 2, 10, 11–
    13, 39, 49, 183
  bird's eye, 34
  figured, 10
  Queen Anne Period, 21
  Sheraton, 34
  tiger, 11–13, 34
  William and Mary Period, 16
Marble
  carved, 4
  tops, Victorian, 43
Marine paintings, 150–151
Marlboro Street Works (Keene,
    N.H.), 63, 64

Marriage chests, 16
Marshall, Nathaniel, 54
Martin, George A., 176
Masonic flasks, 76
Massachusetts
  cabinetmakers (before 1830), 54
  pewterers, 122, 123
  silverwork, 131
  See also specific craftsmen, loca-
    tions, manufacturing com-
    panies, and products
Mather, Reverend Richard, wood-
    cut of, 153
Matisse, Henri, 155
Mayflower, 2
Mead, Abraham, 83
Medicine bottles, 77
Mediterranean-style furniture, 47,
    169
  See also specific countries, items
Mehriban rugs, 164
Mellville, Samuel, 123
Mellville, Thomas, 123
Mellville, William, 123
Merriman, Marcus, 131
Metal dolls, 135–136
Mezzotints, 153
Michigan, 39
Middle Man, The (play), 88
Mile of History, Providence, R.I.,
    8
Military weapons, 168–169
Miniature oil lamps, 159–160
Minott, Samuel, 131
Mirrors, 7, 167
Mission-styled oak furniture, 46–47
Mr. Machine (toy), 145
Molded earthenware, 82
Molds, glass, 71
Mombasa, Kenya, 177–178
Monet, Claude, 146

Moore, N. Hudson, 162
Moran, Thomas, 147
Morris chairs, 4, 6
Morton, George, 89
Moseley, David, 131
Moulton, Joseph, 131
Moulton, William, 131
Moulton family, 131
Mount Lebanon, N.Y., 49
Mt. Washington Glass Works, 61, 68, 72, 73
Muffin tins, 114
Multiboard furniture construction, 14
Mugs
    glass elephant-handle, Nixon-Agnew, 75
    pewter, 121
    silver, 128
Murano (Italy) glass, 79
Museums, 19, 61, 64, 77, 83, 125, 151, 161, 162, 169, 170, 172
    See also specific museums, places
Music boxes, doll, 136
Mystic, Conn., Marine Museum, 151

Nahant, Mass., iron, 111
Nails, furniture, 29, 45
National Association of Dealers in Antiques, 79
National Auctioneers Association, 177
"Near cut" glass, 72
Needlework, 167
Netherlands, see Dutch
New Bedford, Mass., Marine Museum, 151
New England Glass Company, 55, 56, 64, 69, 72

New Granite Glass Works, 63
New Hampshire
    cabinetmakers (before 1830), 13, 26, 54
    Glass Factory, 63
    pewterers, 122
    See also specific craftsmen, locations, products
New York City
    dolls, 138
    furniture craft, 2
New York State, 2, 8, 10, 34, 49, 112
    See also specific craftsmen, items, locations
Newtown, Conn., cabinetmakers, 54
Northwood, Harry, 75
Norton, Captain John, Pottery, 83
Norwich, Conn., cabinetmakers, 54

Oak furniture and furnishings
    Art Nouveau, 4, 5
    Pilgrim Period, 2, 16
    Victorian, 7, 46–47
    William and Mary Period, 16, 19
    See also specific items
Oil lamps, 156–157, 159–160
Oil paintings, 146–152
    artists, 147–149, 151
        See also specific artists
    authenticity, 155
    contemporary, 151, 155
    documentation, 149, 150
    frames, 5, 150
    identification, 149, 150
    as investment, 183
    landscapes, 146, 147–150, 151
    marine, 150–151
    portraits, 146–147

prices (values), 146, 149, 150, 151, 152, 155
reproductions, 153
restoration, 150
still life, 152
Old American Prints (Dreppard), 162
Old China Book, The (Moore), 162
Old Howard Theater, Boston, Mass., 8
Old Saybrook, Conn., cabinet-makers, 54
Olde Town, Chicago, Ill., 8
Oriental brass and copper, 117
Oriental bronzes, 118
Oriental motifs
  Art Nouveau period, 4
  pottery, 88, 94–95
Oriental rugs, 164
Ormolu, 118
Ornaments
  on Pilgrim Period chests, 16
  Queen Anne Period, 21
Otis, Jonathan, 131
Our Pioneer Potters (Clement), 162
Oxblood pottery, 87, 88
Oxblood wool rugs, 164
Oyster-shell
  lamps, 170
  shades, 4

Pad foot legs, 21
Paintings
  on chairs, 149
  oil, *see* Oil paintings
  on Pilgrim "marriage" chests, 16
  on Victorian pine beds, 42
  on wood, 149
  See also Art (artists)

Pairpoint glass, 61, 73
Palace of Fine Arts, Mexico City, 73
Palmer prism glass pattern, 64
Pans
  iron, 115
  tin, 115
Paper dolls, 136–137
Papier-mâché dolls, 137
Parian china, 82, 83, 84
  defined, 82
  dolls, 138
Parke-Bernet Galleries, N.Y.C., 177
Parmelee, Samuel, 131
Patchwork quilts, 165–167
Peachblow glass, 68, 79, 160
Pearl Satinware glass, 68
Pegging construction, 19, 20
Pelham, Peter, 153
Pendulums, clock, 99, 105
Pennsylvania, 10, 34, 88
  See also specific cities and towns, crafts, individuals, manufactured items
Period clothing, 173, 184
Period furniture and furnishings, 13–54
  See also specific craftsmen, items, manufacturers, periods, places, etc.
Period homes, renewed interest in, 6–7
Perkins, Jacob, 131
Perry, Justus, 63
Pewter, 119–125
  care of, 122
  identification of, 120, 121, 123–125
  pewterers, 3, 122–125
  touchmarks, 120, 121, 123–125
  values, 120

Philadelphia, Pa.
  dolls, 138
  furniture, 2, 3, 45
  restorations, 8
  silverwork, 130
Photographs, 162
Phyfe, Duncan, 36–37
Picasso, Pablo, 155
Picture frames, 5, 150
Pictures, 7
  See also Art (artists)
Pierpont, Benjamin, 131
Pig kettles, 113
Pilgrim (Jacobean) Period, 1–2,
    13–16, 82–83, 97
Pilgrims, 1–2, 82–83, 97
  china plates commemorating
    landing of, 97
  See also Pilgrim (Jacobean)
    Period
Pine-wood furniture 2, 10, 39–42,
    183
  construction, 39–42
    See also specific items
  "cottage," 39
  Pilgrim Period, 2
  prices, 183
  Queen Anne Period, 21
  Sheraton Period, 34
  Victorian Period, 39–42
  William and Mary Period, 16,
    19, 20
Pitchers, 84, 88
  art-glass, ix
  hound-handle, 84
Pitkin flask, 63, 76
Pitkin Glass Works, 63
Pittsburgh, Pa., restorations, 7, 8
  Shadyside, 8
Plates
  china, 96–98
  pewter, 121

Plymouth, Mass., 2, 14
Polo, Marco, 80
Pomona glass, 68
Popcorn poppers, 114, 169
Porcelain, 80–98
Porringers, pewter, 121
Porter, Allen, 115, 123
Porter, Freeman, 115, 123
Portland, Me.
  glass, 64, 160
  Museum of Art, 64, 160
  tinware, 115
Portland (Me.) Glass Co., 64
Portrait paintings, 146–147
Portsmouth, N.H.
  cabinetmakers, 54
  Strawberry Banke Restoration, 8
  Warner House, 23
Portugal, imports from, 114
Pots, 113, 115
Potter, Philip, 54
Pottery, 80–98
  Chinese, 84–87, 94–95
  classification, 82
  colors, 81, 89, 95
  decorations (designs), 81, 83–86,
    87–95
  Dedham, 87–88
  Dorchester, 89–94
  history, 83 ff.
  identification, 81, 84–87, 88–89,
    95, 97, 98
  Indian, 1, 82–83
  Keene, 88–89
  markings, 87, 88–89, 97
  Pilgrim, 2, 3
  potters, 3, 83 ff.
  prices (values), 87, 90, 97
  See also specific items, potters,
    places
Potty chairs, 7
Powder horns, 169

Power machinery, use of, 3, 35–36, 39, 52–53
Pratt, Phineas, 14
Press cupboards, 16
Pressed glass, 56 ff., 71
Prices (values), 1, 4, 6, 40, 43, 44, 170–180
  rise in, 1, 4, 6, 7, 125, 127, 128
  tips on, buying antiques, 170–180
Prints, 153–155
Providence, R.I.
  cabinetmakers (before 1830), 54
  Restoration Society, 8
  restorations, 8
Pull toys, 143
Putnam, James, 123

Qali (Oriental rug size), 164
Queen Anne Period, 2–3, 10, 13, 21–26
"Queen's Burmese" (glass), 68
Quilted Satin glass lamps, 160
Quilts, 165–167
Quincy Hall, Boston, Mass., 8

Rabbit-ear chairs, 40
Rabbit motif, pottery, 87, 88
Rag rugs, 163
Railroad watches, 110
Rawson, Joseph, 54
Reading, Mass., iron, 111
Rebecca at the Well pitchers, 84
Re-caning of chairs, 40
Red China, imports from, 94
Redware, 82, 87
Reed, Henry, 123
Renewal programs, urban, 8
Repoussé silverwork, 128
Reproductions, art, 153–155
Restoration, English, 50

Restorations
  period houses and sites, 7–8
  Saugus Iron Works, 111
  villages, 170, 172
Revere, Paul
  engravings, 153
  pewter, 120
  silver, 125, 127, 130
Revolutionary War
  earthenware, 83
  firearms, 168
  furniture and furnishings, 29, 30
  glass, 55
  iron, 112
  tinware, 115
  wooden canteens, 169
Rhode Island
  cabinetmakers, 54
  pewterers, 122, 123
  Pilgrims, 1
  silver, 131
  See also specific cities and towns, items
Ricci, Nando, 89
Richardson, George, 123
Rifles, 168
Riley, Phil M., 162
Rivoire, Apollos, 130
Robertson, Mrs. Emmo, 89
Robertson, Hugh, 87–88
Rochester (N.H.) Agricultural and Mechanical Association country fair, 151
Rockers, 6
  sleighback, 46
  Windsor, 41
Rockinghamware, 83
Rococo style, 52
Rose Amber glass, 68
Rose Medalion ware, 95
Rosewood furniture, 42
Rouse, William, 131

Rowe, Frank, ix, 172, 173, 175
Royal Worcester ware, 88, 95
Rubber dolls, 135
Ruby Amber Ware, 68
Rugs, 163–164
  braided, 163
  embroidered, 163
  hooked, 163
  Oriental, 164
  rag, 163
  "tongue," 163
  tufted, 163
  values (prices), 163, 164

Sailing vessels, paintings of, 150–151
Salem, Mass.
  cabinetmakers, 25, 54
  marine museum, 151
Salisbury, N.H., cabinetmakers, 54
Salisbury, Vt., cabinetmakers, 54
Salt-glazed pottery, 80–81, 89
Samovars, 117
Samplers, needlework, 167
Sandwich drawer pulls, 37
Sandwich Works glass, 56–61, 89
Sargent, John Singer, 147
Satinwood inlays and veneers, 28, 32
Saugus Iron Works, 2, 111
Saws, circular, 48
Schoenhut, Albert, 138
Schoolcraft, Henry, 63, 64
Schuller Museum, N.H., 169
Scollay Square, Boston, Mass., 8
Scotland, stoneware from, 97–98
Scott, Charles, 54
Scrimshaw, 109
Scroddleware, 83
Sea scenes, paintings of, 150–151
Secretary-desks, 23–24

Serpentine design, 43
Settees, 43
  See also Sofas
Sewing machines, 172
Seymour, John, 11, 52–53, 54
Seymour, Thomas, 11, 53, 54
Sgraffito, 81
Shades, glass, 4
Shadyside, Pittsburgh, Pa., 8
Shaker sect, furniture and furnishings of, 48–49
Shakespeare, William, 178, 182
Shang-Yin Period bronzes, 118
Shapleigh, John, 147
Shearer, Thomas, 28
Shelburne Museum, Vt., 77
Shelf clocks, 100, 104
Shelves, 5
Sheraton, Thomas, 10, 13, 28, 29, 32–36
Sheraton Period, 7, 10, 13, 28, 29, 32–36, 183
  See also Federal Period
Ships, paintings of, 150–151
Shotguns, 168
Shows, antique, 151
Side chairs
  Chippendale, 28
  Hepplewhite, 29
Sideboards, 28
Silk fans, 167, 168
Silver- and nickel-plated items, 116, 117
Silverwork, 125–131
  "coin," 131
  documentation, 127
  engraving, 130
  footed, 128
  hand-decorated, 128–130
  as an investment, 183
  remaking, 128

silverworkers, 3, 125, 126–131
sterling, 127, 131
touchmarks, 127
value (prices), 125, 127, 128
Simpkins, William, 131
Singapore, ceramics from, 94
Single-board furniture construction, 39
Skillins, John, 54
Skillins, Samuel, 54
Skillins, Simeon, Jr., 54
Skillins, Simeon, Sr., 54
Skinner, John, 120
Slaves, 10
Sleighback rockers, 46
Sleighs, antique, 184
Smith, Ira, 54
Smith, Joseph L., 87
Smith and Wesson firearms, 168
Sofas
Sheraton, 183
Victorian, 43
Softwoods, 2
See also specific items, woods
Soldiers, toy tin, 135
Somerville, Mass., glass, 72
Sons of Liberty silver bowl, 126
South Amboy, N.J., clay, 89
South Stoddard Glass Co., 63
Southbury, Conn., cabinetmakers, 54
Souvenir china, 183–184
Spain
furniture, 47
pottery, 98
silver, 126
Spangled glass, 69
Spanish-American War firearms, 169
Spanish pine, 19
Spatterware, 68–69

Spinning wheels, 165
Spode, Josiah, 82, 97
Spoons, silver, 131
Sprague, Nathaniel, 63
Springfield, Vt., dolls, 137–138
Springfield firearms, 168
Squared leg furniture construction, 14
Stereopticons, 162–163
Sterling Iron Works, N.Y., 112
Sterling silver, 127, 131
Stevens, J. & E. Co., 141
Stevens, Zachariah, 115
Still-life paintings, 152
Stoddard, N.H., glass, 63, 76
Stoneware, 5, 80–98
Stools, 14
Storage chests, 40
See also Chests
Stoves, 115
Stradivarius instruments, 178
Strawberry Banke Restoration, Portsmouth, N.H., 8
Stuarts (English Restoration), 50
Success to the Railroad flasks, 76
Sugars, silver, 128
Sunburst flasks, 76
Suncook, N.H., glass, 56
Swan, Frank H., Glass Collection, 64
Swords, 169
Synthetics, use of, 48, 169

Tables
banquet, 32
dropleaf, 39, 40
gateleg, 19
Hepplewhite Period, 29–32
kitchen, oak or walnut, 7
marble top, 43
Pilgrim Period, 14

Tables (cont.)
  round dining oak, 5
  Victorian Period, 39, 40, 43
  William and Mary Period, 19
Tabletops, replacement of, 19
Tableware, 128
  See also specific items
Taffeta glass, see Carnival glass
Taft, James S., 88–89
Talking dolls, 136, 138
Tall chests, 15, 16, 21, 145
  See also Chests
Tall (grandfather) clocks, 100,
    101, 102, 103, 104, 105
Tall (spinning) wheels, 165
"Tallboys," 21
  See also Chests
Tankards, silver, 128, 130
Tea caddies, silver, 128
Tea sets
  pottery, 88, 90
  silver, 125, 128
  See also Teapots
Teapots, 116, 117, 121, 128
  See also Tea sets
Temple, N.H., glass, 5
Temple, Shirley, paper doll, 137
Terry, Eli, 101, 103
Thomas, Seth, 101, 103, 106
Thompson, Martha, 140
Thompson, Murray, 140
Thumb-back chairs, 40
Tiffany, Louis Comfort, 4, 72–75
  bronzes, 4, 73, 118
  Curtain, 73
  desk sets, 73
  glass, 4, 72–75
  lamps, 4, 73
  markings, 73
  vases, 170
Tiger maple wood, 11–13, 34

Tilt-top game tables, 29, 34
Tin
  banks, 141, 142
  canteens, 169
  soldiers, 135, 143
  toys, 135, 143
  See also Tinware
Tintypes, 162
Tinware, 115
  decorated, 115
  and pewter, 119–120
  prices, 113
  See also Tin
Toasters, iron-rack, 114
Tomahawk heads, 1
Tongue rugs, 163
Tools
  antique, 173
  fireplace, 113, 114, 115, 116
  power, use of, 3, 35–36, 39, 52–
    53
Touchmarks
  pewter, 120, 121, 123–125
  silver, 127
  See also specific craftsmen,
    items, manufacturers, places
Towel holders, 5
Town houses, 6–8, 39
Townsend family, 11, 53, 54
Towzell, John, 131
Toys, 138, 143–146
  See also Banks; Dolls
Train sets, 144
Transitional period pieces, 24
Trask, Israel, 123
Trask, Oliver, 123
Tree-of-life glass pattern, 64
Treenware, 120–121
Trenchers, pewter, 121
Trunks, 40
Tufted rugs, 163

Twin Forts of Popolopen Creek, iron chain at, 112–113
Tyler, Andrew, 131

Union Glass Works, Somerville, Mass., 72
Utensils, metal, 114, 115, 120, 131
  See also specific items
Utility earthenware, 82

Valentine's Day cards, 144
Vasa Murrhina glass, 69
Vases, 5
  glass, 56
  Oxblood pottery, 87, 88
  Tiffany, 170
Veneers and inlays, 10–13, 53
  Adam brothers, 28
  Centennial, 45
  Chippendale, 26
  Sheraton Period, 34, 35
  Victorian Period, 42–43
  William and Mary Period, 16
Vermont
  cabinetmakers (before 1830), 54
  glass, 63–64
  pewterers, 122
  pottery, 82–87
  stoneware, 82, 84–87
Vermont Glass Works, 63–64
Victoria, Queen, 68
Victorian Period, 13, 39–54
  art-glass, ix, 68
  copper and brass, 116–117
  furniture and furnishings, 7, 39–54
  houses, 6, 7
  prices (values), 32
  See also specific items
Villages, restoration of, 170, 172
Virginia, 10, 21

Wadsworth Atheneum, Hartford, Conn., 83, 162
Waffle bakers, 114
Wagons, antique, 184
Waldegrave, Lord, 177
Walker, Izannah, 138
Walking dolls, 136
Wall clocks, 105
Walnut-wood furniture, 7, 10, 42, 47
  Queen Anne Period, 10, 21, 23
  Victorian Period, 42
  William and Mary Period, 16, 19
Walpole, Horace, 177
Waltham watches, 104
War of 1812, 3
Ward, William, 131
Warner House, Portsmouth, N.H., secretary-desk, 23
Washing machines, 48
Washington, Mount, landscape paintings, 149–150
Washstand sets, 5
Watches (watchmaking), 104–105, 109
  gold, 110
  key-wind, 109–110
  railroad, 110
  See also Clocks
Waterbury watches, 104
Wax dolls, 134–135
Weapons, military, 168–169
Weathervanes, 113, 116
Weaver, William, 54
Wedgwood china, 97
Weights, clock, 99–101, 103, 104
West Willington (Conn.) Glass Works, 63
Westbrook, Me., decorated tin-ware, 115

Wetting dolls, 136
Whale-oil lamps, 113, 159
Whieldon, Thomas, 97
Whistler, James, 147
White Mountain School artists, 147, 149–150
Whitmore, Jacob, 123
Whitney, Eli, 168
Wild Rose glass, 68
Willard, Aaron, 106
Willard, Simon, 103, 104, 106
William and Mary Period, 13, 16–21, 24, 52
    See also specific items
Winchester firearms, 168
Window glass, 2, 55, 63, 71
Windsor chairs, 41–42
Wing, Bliss and Harper banks, 141
Winslow, Edward, 131
Winthrop, Me., cabinetmakers, 54
Wood, paintings on, 149
Woodcarver of Salem, The (Cousins and Riley), 162

Wood-carving and woodcarvers, see Carvings (carvers)
Woodcuts, 153
Wooden canteens, 169
Wooden clock movements, 100–101
Wooden dolls, 134, 138
Woodenware (wooden utensils), 120–121
Woods, 10–13, 34, 42
    See also specific items, periods, kinds of wood
Wool
    bed coverings, 164–165, 167
    rugs, 163, 164
Woolworth Building iron banks, 143
Worcester ware, 88, 95
Worktables, 40

Yeaton, Mrs., 89
Young, David, 106

Zinc, use of, 116